EYEBALL TO EYEBALL

by

Tom, Patricia and Michael Askwith

CONTENTS

CHAPTER

PART 1 AFGHANISTAN

1	GETTING THERE	7
2	FIRST SIGHT	11
3	KABUL	15
4	THE PEOPLES OF AFGHANISTAN	21
5	PHYSICIAN HEAL THYSELF	29
6	GULZAR	37
7	FOREIGNERS	47
8	CAUTIONARY TALES	55
	A. VIP'S	55
	B. I WISH TO SERVE MY COUNTRY	61
	C. LOCAL COMMENTS	64
	D. THE VERDICT	66
9	COMMUNITY DEVELOPMENT	69
10	THE SELANG TUNNEL	73
11	THE GREAT GRAPE AIRLIFT	77
12	MEMORIES OF AFGHANISTAN	83

PART 2 TURKEY

13	THE SICK MAN OF EUROPE	91
14	FINDING A WAY	101
15	PATRICIA'S DIARY	111
16	WHIRLING DERVISHES	117
17	ON THE HIPPY TRAIL	123
18	MEMORIES OF TURKEY	153

APPENDIX A

COMMUNITY DEVELOPMENT AND LOCAL GOVERNMENT	161
COMMUNITY DEVELOPMENT IN TURKEY	168
THE BACKGROUND	169
THE FIRST STEP	169
VILLAGE INSTITUTES	170
AGRICULTURAL EXTENSION	170
THE PROMOTION OF RURAL DEVELOPMENT	170
ADULT EDUCATION AND COMMUNITY DEVELOPMENT	171
THE FIVE YEAR PLAN	171
SPONTANEOUS SCHEMES OF COMMUNITY DEVELOPMENT	171
THE PROBLEMS	172
EXAMPLES OF PROGRAMMES	173
THE LESSONS LEARNT	175
THE MINISTRY OF VILLAGE AFFAIRS	176

GLOSSARY   177

N.B. The names of the individuals which appear in the anecdotes in various parts of the book are of course fictitious and must not be taken too literally.

LIST OF ILLUSTRATIONS

	PAGE
Map	6
The Giant Buddhas of Bamian	21
Road to Jellalbad	83
Bandi Amir Salt Lake	87
Map	90
Ankara Castle	91
Samsun	104
Seljuk Bridge	108
Aegea, Roman Amphitheatre	110
Aegea, The Mediterranean Coastline	110
Kursadasi	112
Glades near Bursa	114
Caravanserai near Konya	117
The Taurus Mountains	129
Seljuk Citadel near Ephesus	151

PART 1

AFGHANISTAN

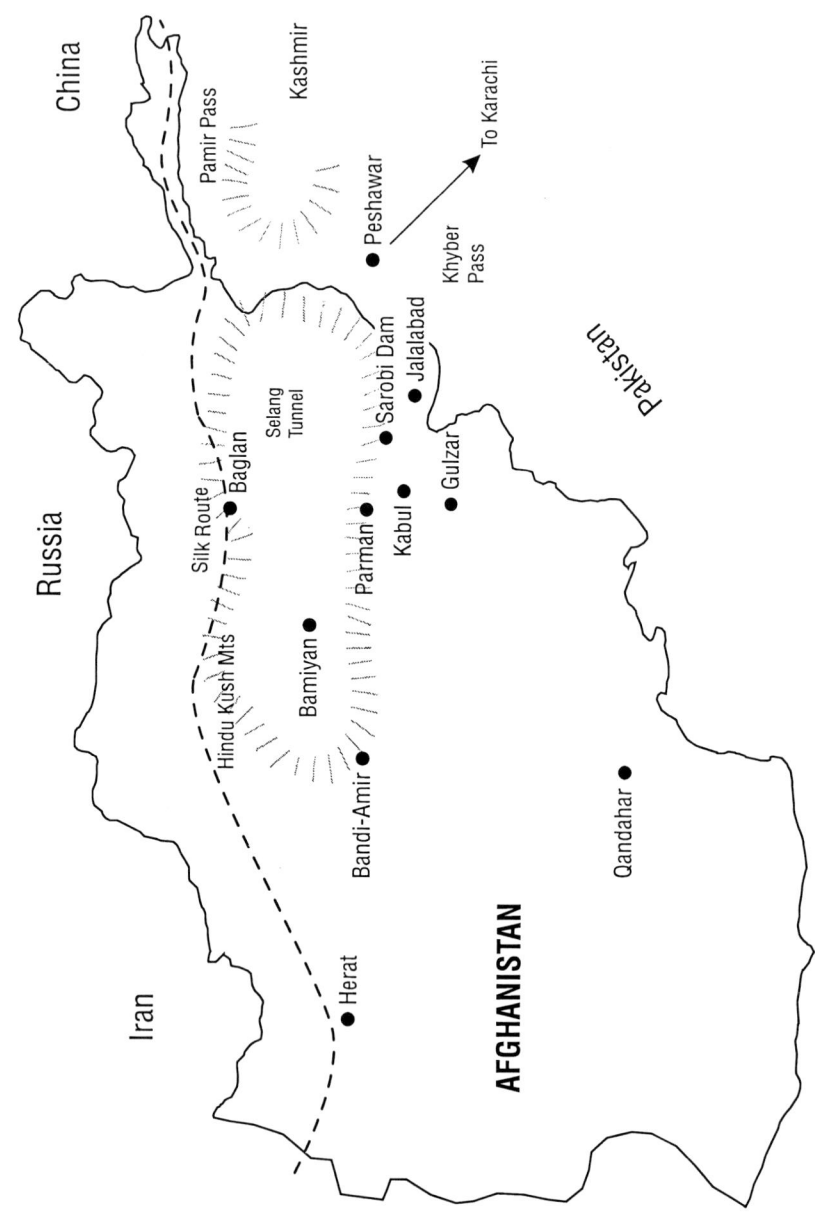

CHAPTER 1

Getting There

BY TOM

The Union Jack was shortly to be lowered at the Independence celebrations in Uhuru Park in Nairobi and as it happened soon after I was due to retire at what I regarded the ridiculously early age of 50. It was of course a hang-up from the days when 25 years of service in the tropics was regarded as virtually a life sentence. One could expect a few years of ambling golf, followed by a few more of gardening in some quiet country village is not so different to what so many fortunate business men have to go through when they receive their redundancy notice these days.

But I suppose I was lucky. Having specialised in a comparatively obscure method of promoting rapid progress in under-developed countries known as Community Development during the latter part of my service, I was offered a post by the United Nations Development Programme in a country which seemed to be almost as retarded economically as was Kenya when we had first arrived there a quarter of a century earlier. I can't say I exactly jumped at the idea, but there seemed to be rather more prospects of a novel form of lifestyle than we had so far experienced. Apart from that the pay was good and the children were at a very expensive stage of their education. Patricia was always ready to try something new and the prospect of life in Little Pudlington was quite as unattractive to her as it was to me. The children needless to say were somewhat appalled by the idea of life "out there" which was how they described England, even though it had to be endured during term time. The reality was to be even more remarkable than we were led to believe by a study of the otherwise admirable job description provided by the United Nations.

We gathered that the roads in Afghanistan were not much worse than those we had grown accustomed to in Kenya, so we shipped the Peugeot off to Karachi, little knowing that that was the last we would see of her for the next nine months. We took advantage of our entitlement to employ professional packers and I booked my flight to Kabul, having I am ashamed to say, searched for it on the map for the first time. It was to be quite an eye-opener.

Eyeball to Eyeball

Patricia on the other hand set off for England with the children to put them into their respective schools and join me in due course in Afghanistan which was quite a saga in its own right.

So in due course I found myself bound for Kabul. But before that I had been instructed to call in at the UN area office which was situated in Bangkok some 2000 miles to the East for briefing. Joining the UN seemed an excellent way of seeing the world, or at any rate its airports, which were all somewhat similar, apart from their sanitary facilities.

Five sleepless hours later I unwound myself from the cramped seat and extracted luggage from under my feet and the lockers and recesses beside the seat and staggered out into the stifling damp of Thailand.

The receptionist at the UN office looked at me with blank mystification. The importance of my visit had obviously not filtered down to her level and the next thing was to find someone who had heard about this auspicious event. In due course another flustered lady appeared full of apologies.

"You must forgive me Mr Askwith" pronounced as in "Task" with a broad American accent. "I am afraid particulars of your visit have got mislaid".

I assured her it was of no significance and explained that the head office of UNTB (everything is known by its prefixes in International circles, although unfortunately no dictionary of their significance had yet been compiled), thought that I should be briefed about Afghanistan before taking up my appointment. Perhaps I should be introduced to whoever it was who was responsible for the programme. The lady looked at me in even more embarrassment. "Sure, Mr Askwith, you are quite right". There was a long pause while she covered her confusion by peering at her papers.

"The difficulty is that the officer in charge of the Afghanistan desk is at present" - another pause - "in Korea" - another pause "and he won't be back for a couple of weeks".

The truly global nature of my new appointment began to dawn upon me as well as the fragility of the system of communications. There was apparently no one else in the office who had any knowledge of Afghanistan whatsoever.

"I suggest that you should make the best of your visit to Bangkok and see the sights. You will find it a fascinating city and you mustn't miss the floating market".

Getting There

I had no doubt of this. Tourists paid hundreds of pounds for such an opportunity and I was obviously extremely lucky. Three days and a dozen golden temples later and I was again soaring over Central Asia towards the almost mythical land of Alexander, Tammerlane, and Genghis Khan. It was all beginning to get exciting.

They told us that fortunately the DC3 of Aryan Afghan Airways would be leaving for Kabul the next day. The Schedule of flights was controlled by the extent of cloud over the mountains, but fortunately visibility was expected to be good and the pilot should be able to find his way through the passes to the 5000 foot plateau above. We should get a good view of the rugged countryside as we bumped our way into the interior.

I was not disappointed, as we climbed over ridge after ridge of dessicated hills one could appreciate how a lunar landscape might appear. Every strata of rock, bare of any vestige of vegetation except in the valley bottoms stood out clean and evenly defined, brown, yellow, orange, even purple in places. In the far distance was the great bastion of the snow covered Hindu Kush where the Himalayas peter out in the deserts of Iran.

I jammed my elbow against the window to try to stop it rattling and the draught blowing down my neck, which at last was beginning to feel refreshingly cool, and peered below us as vivid strips of turquoise appeared in the bottom of valleys, where dams had been constructed and narrow threads of roadway twisted like snakes across the plains and up the escarpment. Little ochre villages with flat roofs surrounded by emerald patches of irrigated cultivation were strung like beads along them.

We had left the plains and the great Cities of the Punjab behind us and in due course could just make out the historic route through the Khyber Pass, down which so many invading armies had passed on their way to plunder the riches of India.

From the air one could begin to see this historic panorama in perspective. Situated like a bastion at the western end of that formidable barrier separating China from India lay the Pamir Pedicle, the only pass in its North East corner. To the west, giving access to Russia and skirting the Hindu Kush, to the North West, the road to Iran through Herat; lastly the historic route to the Indies through the Khyber Pass to the South.

The first known invaders, all of whom used Afghanistan as the gateway to India, were the Greeks, under Alexander the Great, who entered from Herat in the

Eyeball to Eyeball

North. The next were the Monguls who came through the Pamir in the North East, and they were followed by successive waves of Nomads including Tamarlaine (Timur Ling). Finally, rivalry between Britain and Russia led to a succession of wars ending with the recent invasion by Russia which provides the backdrop to my tale.

In the process, the cities of Afghanistan suffered almost continual destruction and were constantly being rebuilt. In the course of our years sojourn in this huge country we were only able to visit a part of it, as of course we were not tourists but employed to try to make a small contribution to what seemed an almost endless process of reconstruction.

So as our plane hopped over the rim of the saucer in which Kabul is situated, the road to Russia and the North stretched out ahead of us, branching off to Iran or China beyond the Hindu Kush as the case might be.

The old airport was barely distinguishable from the surrounding desert but beyond it the huge new buildings of the new one were still under construction. Had I realised it at the time, they marked the site of one of the strangest episodes in the recent history of Afghanistan - the great-grape-airlift as it might be called.

We landed without incident in a cloud of dust, which was a foretaste of things to come. Everything seemed to occur in a cloud of dust. It would be surprising if it were otherwise for it scarcely ever rained and all its mighty rivers were fed by the melting snows which fell on the Hindu Kush during the winter months.

We walked over to the air terminus, a row of single storied flat roofed brick buildings which only opened on the rare occasions that an aircraft happened to arrive. Some months later I was to return to them to try to find out when Patricia's plane from Beirut was due to arrive.

CHAPTER 2

First Sight

BY TOM

As we approached the ancient town we began to take in its shape and layout. First in the outskirts the broad boulevards and modern houses. Next the less smart but recently laid out suburbs with the traditional juis or watercourses running down each side of the street. These supplied water for the houses for washing or drinking. Having an immunity to most common ailments including typhoid, the local people did not have to worry about purifying their drinking water.

These rows of flat roofed houses gave way to streets in the same style except that they were fitted out as shops and piled high, either with brilliantly coloured piles of fruit with grapes hanging from the ceiling, or stacked with ironmongery such as stoves or pots and pans, or materials. The only difference between these shops and our own was that they follow the oriental and our own mediaeval tradition, each street tend to specialise in one particular trade. The only exceptions to this practise were the bakeries for "non unleavened" bread. "Nan".

The first time I saw an Afghan with a thick beard and turban, its loose end hanging down over his chest, walking towards me reverently carrying something covered with a cloth, I thought it must be a baby. But I was wrong. It was his household's daily requirements of Nan. He had just collected it from the bakery which as often as not simply consisted of a counter set in a wall over which the oval slabs of bread were slid steaming and smelling, crusty and delicious. If one peered inside one could just see the opening to the oven glowing in the floor. The soft uncooked dough was slapped on to the red hot walls and started to bake immediately. At the psychological moment, they were scooped off the side of the oven with a wooden shovel and swung directly on to the counter.

Next to the stove another baker was shaping fresh dough into the traditional shape while being kneaded with the hands and finger nails. But it must be placed

Eyeball to Eyeball

on the table with the minimum of delay as freshness and heat were all important. Bakeries were therefore scattered fairly thickly around the residential areas.

And so in due course we found our way, weaving round the pot holes, putting hens to flight and avoiding donkeys, their panniers loaded to the brim with succulent apples or oranges on their way to supply the shops.

Meanwhile, there was an incessant sound of shouting, for Afghans have loud voices, no doubt developed to make themselves heard from mountaintop to mountaintop. Since the winter was approaching, the men were beginning to wear their kaftans, long quilted coats with appropriately long sleeves into which one could withdraw ones hands for warmth, thus dispensing with the need for gloves. The more affluent men wore astrakhan caps made of the skin of an unborn lamb and consequently quite expensive. They were known as karrakuls, always made to measure by a hat maker; some grey, some brown and others even black.

It was somewhat a sensation to see all the women clad in light garments known as chadri which completely covered them and were fitted with a mesh opening, through which they would peer. An Afghan man would never see a woman's face except perhaps in the country, where it would be quite impossible to work in such a garment, or in the privacy of ones home. When one did have the honour to be a guest of an Afghan family, one found that under their chadris they were splendidly attired in beautiful dresses, shoes and much jewellery.

Much of Kabul has now been destroyed in the battles which have raged over the years, and no doubt it has happened countless times in the past. One advantage of the mudbuilt buildings is that they are not difficult to repair and the builders can never lack employment.

A feature of life in Kabul was the way that nothing was wasted. Every baked bean tin was kept and a handle fixed to the side to convert it to a mug. Rugs are woven, or furniture made from local poplar trees and so forth. This is not surprising as all imports have to come in on trucks from Pakistan. Afghans are remarkable craftsmen and if a spare part to ones car is not available they would make it or adapt it from some crashed vehicle. An intensely warlike people there was a great demand for firearms which if in short supply they manufactured for themselves.

As strict Muslims, they were teetotal but sipped large quantities of green tea from little glasses shaped like thistles with a waist which caught the tea leaves and prevented them going down ones throat. Teashops were everywhere in the

First Sight

towns and villages and along the main roads. They were referred to as chaikhanas, pronounced Chayhonas and were as much an institution as the English Pub. The water was boiled in a large samovar which sat on the counter and puffed out steam when the water boiled.

The general impression given was that the way of life of the inhabitants was not unlike that which must have prevailed in the Middle Ages throughout Europe. We would not have gone in for flat roofs because of our heavy rainfall but our cob walls were not unlike the Afghan variety. We would have had juis running down the sides of our streets - they still exist in Trumpington Street in Cambridge. We would have thrown our slops into the street too. Our clothes were not so different either. Turbans were worn by Rembrandt as we know from his self portraits and men wore cloaks, not unlike kaftans, and men rode horses or donkeys while little boys swept up their droppings for use as manure and everyone went armed, although actual street fighting was rare. Mosques were as common as city churches. We were both ruled by Kings, though that is now a thing of the past in Afghanistan.

Our year was punctuated by festivals, many of them fixed according to the time of year, though in Europe adopted as part of the Christian Calendar, while in Afghanistan, Muslim festivals have always remained separate from seasonal ones.

But as one moved through the streets, one could not help noticing the many similarities which existed between the way of life of present day Afghans and that of our own mediaeval ancestors. This even extended to furniture which was largely non existent, even to the extent of sleeping on rush-covered floor coverings round the fire.

But a remarkable similarity of physical characteristics were also noticeable. Our complexions under the Afghan suntan were basically the same as were our features, our hair and beards, if we wore them, and the colours of our eyes and even our languages as we shall see later, were often similar.

But in fact there were many racial divisions within the population which were largely due to the successive invasions which had left their mark on their descendants throughout the country. We were very surprised to find when we learned more about the inhabitants that though these incursions had taken place many hundreds if not thousands of years ago, the ethnic characteristics of the different periods still remained and could be identified, if sometimes rather dimly. But let us take them in turn.

CHAPTER 3

Kabul

BY PATRICIA ON ARRIVAL

My first impressions of Kabul seem a bit hazy, as I was so tired that first day after having been awake all night. After a long wait at the airport, sitting on my luggage in the shade of the customs shed, waiting for Tom to meet me, I gave up and took the Ariana bus into the town, more or less the only passenger, as the others had disappeared on arrival. I was deposited at the Kabul Hotel, and I went to the reception desk to ask if I could ring up somebody at the United Nations Headquarters. As I was struggling to make the clerk understand, a large Canadian came to my rescue and asked if he could help. Thankfully I said yes, and he managed to get on to someone and a message was left to say I had arrived. A little later George Humphreys (the Administrator) arrived and whirled me off to the bazaar. We stopped in the middle of a crowded street, humming with noise, before some battered high green gates. On pulling the bell rope, a small door in the big one opened and we were ushered into a compound. And there was Tom, vastly surprised to see me as he had been told that there couldn't be another plane for several days. He had gone to meet me the day before, but no luck, so had had to eat the fatted calf (in this case a chicken) prepared for my benefit, and await developments. I was thankful to see him, and by this time was so tired that the rest of the day passed in a sort of daze. After lunch we went for a drive out of the city towards the dam, but afterwards I had no recollection of this at all, and didn't recognise it when taken there again. A good nights sleep was all that was necessary though.

Our house was unimpressive at first, or indeed at any time. The back wall of it faced directly on the street, the compound being square, with high mud walls all round it. There were three rooms in a row, bedroom, dining/cum sitting room and kitchen with a verandah in front. All the outside woodwork was painted a hideous yellow ochre, with dark grey outer walls. Inside was whitewashed, and the door and furniture were made of varnished badly seasoned wood with wide cracks everywhere. The varnish smelt of incense, and I have not met it anywhere else; it is a peculiarly Afghan smell.

Eyeball to Eyeball

The furniture was largely inherited from the Frenchman who owned the house previously, plus some chairs and a settee made in native style to Tom's measurements, with cushions made from donkey bags stuffed with kapok. They looked most gay, purples and black and orange, and were suprisingly comfortable, and much better than the pseudo European furniture made and sold in the furniture shops, whose life was short and second hand value low after a few years. The kitchen was austere, with a tap and sink, and a shelf on which was the electric stove - a Baby Belling, with which Abdul worked wonders. Everything had to be covered at night owing to the mice. Abdul, the cook/houseboy had also been inherited along with the house, and was a small wizened man of indeterminate age, who mostly spoke pidgin French. His favourite English phrase was "Zis no good". He did all the shopping very economically. But his cooking was monotonous. He liked to prepare vast mountains of pilau, or stew, and "compote" of fruit, and serve them up for every meal until they were finished, and could not understand why we should want something different for each meal, a very non-laboursaving idea. He lived out and bicycled to work each day, arriving about 7am, and left again about 5pm as we preferred to have the evening to ourselves.

The garden consisted of bare brown earth and a few wisps of old brown grass at this time of the year, at the end of February, and there were still piles of dirty unmelted snow from the winter. Very soon a few green shoots would appear and the whole scene would change rapidly, but my first impressions were of a khaki landscape, no colour anywhere except for the vivid blue sky, and the mountains covered with snow which surrounded the town. There was a big bald brown hill almost leaning over the town, and those who lived right under it found it got them down, and felt it to be too oppressive. But we were not too near. Within our purdah walls we could feel entirely private once we had gone through our green gates and could forget the teeming bazaar just outside. But once one stepped through the gate one was right in the thick of city life. There were shops on each side of the road, a couple of grocers, greengrocers, a butcher, a hairdresser and a teapot mender, whose shop sign was a line of teapot spouts strung on a line hung up in front. Also a shop which sold some kind of fat in large tins, for which people queued up. At the corner was a kind of large caravan affair, which sold "Turkish" bread - long loaves of proper bread, as opposed to Afghan unleavened bread. This is called 'nan' and is regarded as almost holy - one must never ever throw it away or waste it. It comes in flat thin pieces shaped like a snow shoe, with perforations all over it which we discovered were made by the bakers' finger nails. There were nan shops in every road, and a delicious smell would pervade the air when they were baking. In the winter it looked a cosy job, with the nan being cooked on the inside of

Kabul

the mud ovens and the flames roaring below, but in summer it must have been hell.

I never grew tired of watching the life in the streets and would enjoy being left in the car while Tom went off to work. There was always so much to see and the people so colourfully dressed. The modern younger men would be dressed in neat suits and karakol hats and be very smartly turned out, with the girls in short modern skirts and bouffant hair styles. But the ordinary man in the street would wear a waistcoat over a very long shirt reaching almost to his heels, and very baggy trousers. On his head would be a turban, not very neatly tied with a long tail, which would be useful for so many things, protection from dust and flies and for wiping the eyes and, or, nose. In winter they would wear long padded overcoats the outside made of striped silk or cotton, and the inside always lined with flowered material with a small design. On Fridays these would be very decorative. The sleeves were immensely long, but usually the coat would be worn casually across the shoulders. I think the long sleeves were designed so that the hands could be tucked into them for warmth. The village types would have long flowing beards but the modern man was mostly clean shaven. There was a fascinating mixture of types too, slanting eyed Mongolians who were mostly the load carriers and menial labourers, and the tall upstanding tribesmen with fair skins and blue eyes, and very good looking.

Most of the women would never venture out of their homes unless shrouded from head to foot with the Chadri, a tent like covering with a few rows of embroidered holes to see out of. Underneath you would often see glimpses of nylon stockings and high heeled shoes, not to mention white gloves, but it was not polite to look at them too closely and forbidden to take photographs. The chadris were mostly made of pleated silk, in pleasantly mellow colours of blue and red and green, not just the black you see in other countries. One was not supposed to take them out of the country, though we did manage to bring one home. Ones luggage was closely searched when going out, as well as coming in, in case one was smuggling out karakol skins, or anything else considered detrimental to the image of the country as an advanced nation.

The donkey was the most useful form of transport and used for everything. They and the horses must have had a hard time, yet the owners were obviously quite fond of them in their way. Most horses pulling gharis wear blinkers and have red bobbles all over their bridles. Sometimes a horse will have a nylon net scarf tied round its neck or tied in a bow under its chin, and on special occasions a head scarf round its forehead, or even a balloon tied to the halter. Lorries are treated the same way. The lorry-cum-bus is of distinctly old fashioned build, very square, with a wide platform on either side of the bonnet, possibly for the "engineer" to sit on, or in summer for the overflow of passengers. Every square inch of the outside is painted in many colours and designs, mostly of fabulous beasts and birds and schlosses on the Rhine, lakes with swans and so forth. Inside, the cab, which looks hideously uncomfortable, very upright and narrow, is decorated in similar fashion. Along the inside of the windscreen is a row of bobbles and streamers through which the driver and passengers peer out with difficulty, usually some vases of plastic flowers along the bottom, while on the outside there may be some folded silk handkerchiefs stretched across as on a horses brow. Bobbles and streamers also flutter out of the side windows, and from a car behind they are apt to look like hands giving strange signals. Passengers are crammed inside and on the roof to saturation point, and as many as possible squashed in on each side of the driver. In the summer the bonnet casing would be removed entirely to keep the engine cool. One practically never saw a new bus or lorry, they were nearly all home-made and the bodies perhaps constructed from some other wrecked bus, and the engine parts cannibalised.

Home Sweet Home (by Tom)

Deciding to rent a house and actually finding one were two very different things. There were of course no such things as Estate Agents, but the various organisations concerned with the employment of foreigners kept lists of suitable dwellings and it was then just a matter of going round to visit them in the hope that they would live up to ones expectations.

Only the Americans and diplomats could afford to rent houses up to the standards of middle class families in England. Not that they were anything like English houses. They were absolutely traditional and standard. A roughly square plot with the single storied house on the road side, surrounded by a ten foot "purdah" wall a "jui" or irrigation canal flowed under one corner of this wall and out at the opposite one, following a zigzag pattern between the houses. The garden, if there was one, was bounded by the flat roofed house on the road side, and the other three purdah walls, square with a lawn in the middle and flower beds on the other sides which resembled the design of a persian garden or perhaps the other way round. We had not realised before that this design represented rose trees or other flowers in a garden. There was often a pergola which ran along the walls and carried festoons of delicious grapes in autumn and gave refreshing shade in the heat of summer.

What I have to say is really supplementary to what Patricia has already written but from a rather different point of view.

Kabul

Housing to rent to foreigners was the main source of income for Afghans in the top income brackets. In fact one sometimes felt that they would not have had much interest in foreign aid without it. The perks of foreign travel and bursaries were of course acceptable but comparatively insignificant. This class of affluent Afghan naturally kept the best houses for themselves and employed contractors to build special European-type houses for letting purposes. Left to themselves they would probably have lived in traditional style, sleeping on the mattress round the traditional or semi traditional bokhari which I suppose was German in origin, with all feet pointing inwards in a great circle.

One most attractive feature of the traditional houses was that they mostly had gul khanas or conservatories at one corner. The tender plants from the garden were brought in there in wintertime and they gave off a strong and sometimes rather suffocating scent, especially the geraniums. But the sunshine which poured in out of the clear blue winter skies was most stimulating.

Patricia has not mentioned some of the other duties for which Mohammet was responsible. It was his job to convert the coal dust, whose arrival in the middle of a dinner party she has described, into briquettes. This he did in the coal shed which was conveniently situated next to the water pump. He had to spend many days patting them into convenient shapes for loading into the bokhari and then stacking them to dry because they were very brittle.

In summer he became the gardener which included watering the plants from our section of the jui. When we first moved into our house, which Patricia and I chose together, there was no garden as the house was comparatively new, but we thought it would be rather nice to have something to look out on from the sitting room instead of piles of builders rubble which we found when we first arrived from the temporary dwelling, had rented when I decided to get out of the hostel and its insanitary water supply.

I therefore made some enquiries from my colleagues as to how best to make myself a garden. They told me there were expert garden planners who would be very happy to do it for me and in due course they knocked on my door one morning and said they had come to make a garden for me. This was before Patricia arrived.

The party consisted of two chaps with the traditional long handled shovels and two donkeys on whose backs were loaded enormous sacks of what looked like chaff and two large reels of string. First they began, apparently with no measuring instruments, to lay out the flower beds like giant window frames. Then they shovelled out the bed of the jui and the earth outwards to form the

Eyeball to Eyeball

surrounding flowerbeds. Finally they leveled the intervening lawn in the centre and planted vines against the walls.

The time had come to open the sluice gate of the jui and allow the water to enter the newly dug trench. The men then scooped out the water and scattered it all over the "lawn" and leveled it carefully with their feet as if they were paddling on the sea shore.

Now all we had to do was ask the gardener to water it twice a day and in two weeks it would sprout and become a lawn. Suprisingly enough that was exactly what happened.

The next thing was to plant flowers and they told me all we had to do was to go down to the market and pick out the flowers we liked and again get Mohammet to plant them and of course water them. Mohammet knew all about that and in no time they had begun to spread and grow. Vine seedlings or cuttings followed and by the end of the summer we had acquired a cheerful landscape in place of a quarry.

Later that summer we had a grand opening. There was a platform that foreigners could hire when they threw a party and put it up in the garden. When the children came out for the holidays we organised a dance and borrowed a record player. The party went on far into the night and we hoped our neighbours were not too disturbed by the noise, but if they were they were far too polite to complain.

CHAPTER 4

The Peoples of Afghanistan

BY TOM

The Giant Buddhas of Bamian

I suppose when one first studies a map of the country one imagines a vast saucer bounded on the north by the snow-capped mountains of the Hindu Kush. The land drops steeply into the fertile plains of the Punjab in Pakistan on the eastern side and more gradually into the plains and deserts of Iran on the west.

It is occupied not by one race of people but no less than four, distinguished more by their countries of origin and occupations than their racial characteristics, for they all look and are clothed much alike except for the city dwellers, who usually wore "Karakol" hats made from the pelts of unborn lambs. Apart from this they were clad in Kaftans, which looked like long striped dressing gowns, padded in winter with sleeves which covered the hands.

Eyeball to Eyeball

As to their racial characteristics and languages one should firstly list the Pachtu, referred to as the Pathans in the old days of the British Raj. At their head was the King, until the dissolution of the monarchy after the Russian invasion, and their homeland was in the mountains like the Highland Scots and were split into numerous clans which were constantly at war with each other.

Like a number of middle-eastern countries there existed a continuous state of rivalry between the regular and civil authorities. The country people supported the priests or mullahs and were fiercely conservative, whereas the king and the large landowners represented the forces of change.

"Jeshan", which was celebrated at spring time, epitomised the new year and like the christian birth of Christ marked the fertility of mankind at the melting of the snows.

The king often drew attention to the period by introducing some significant reform. When we attended in 1962 we naturally appeared at the big agricultural show held in the stadium. He appeared with the Queen and his daughters, all of whom were unveiled, an unheard of innovation at the time and an implied criticism of the priesthood.

It was an act of considerable bravery on his part but had the support of the progressives in the country who admired the reforms undertaken by the Russians across the border to the north. We shall see later that the Soviet Union played this card when it decided to invade Afghanistan. It did not win the trick however. The Nationalists in Afghanistan resisted the might of their neighbour as they did later in Vietnam and in most of Africa.

We shall see later how great has been the unifying force of Islam throughout Central Asia since its introduction, Communism alone has offered a comparable influence.

We shall see a similar tendency in the case of Turkey in due course, where the Government had to choose between the counter attractions of Communism or Capitalism.

On my first drive to Gulzar, the training centre 10 miles outside Kabul to which I was attached, I noticed that all the low walls which separated the paddy fields beside the road had been demolished. I asked the reason for this and was told that it was to reduce the cover they afforded to snipers, which seemed to me to be a laudable intention. No official census had been undertaken, but the Pushtu were believed to number about 4 million. They are thought to have originated

The Peoples of Afghanistan

in Persia. The prophet Ezra refers to ten tribes who fled to "Arsathereth" and this may have given the present day "Hazaras" their name. The young men who formed the course I was entrusted with in Gulzar were members of this tribe. On the other hand about a million Mongols living in the interior of the country are also referred to as Hazara but they speak Farsi so the situation is confusing. To make matters worse they had the status of slaves and still are engaged as porters of heavy loads such as articles of furniture, fridges and such like from house to house in Kabul.

Another most interesting section of the population were the "Kaffirs", or Infidels, who number less than a million and live in the north west corner of the country in an area known as Land of Light or "Nuristan". Like the Pachtu they are fair skinned and some believe they are descended from members of the army of Alexander the Great on his campaign to India in the third century BC.

We happened to pick up a rug which depicted scenes of Afghan life including men and women on horseback, hawking, household objects like tea pots, an Afghan hound, partridges, and so on. It was interesting, as Muslim law forbids the portrayal of the human figure and we wondered whether it was the work of Kaffir craftsmen.

The largest tribe in the country are the Persians or Iranians who number about the same as the Pachtu at 4 million. They speak Farsi and represent the commercial and agricultural communities who live in the north west and northern areas and in Kabul their language is naturally spoken widely.

There are people from a variety of neighbouring countries such as Turkmemistan, Uzbecistan and Tartary living in the north and Kabul areas. But the most fascinating people in Afghanistan were the Kuchis. They were the true nomads who spent the winter in Pakistan and the summer harvesting the crops of the Pachtus.

On one of our expeditions into the countryside, we were having a picnic under one of the few shade trees in the area. The spring sunshine had begun to warm the mountain air and ripen the fields of wheat. In the distance a string of Great Bachtrian, two humped dromedaries, was approaching in a majestic manner. Each of the great beasts was loaded with black tents, poles and guy ropes with bags of domestic belongings tied to every convenient obtrusion. The whole was covered with wide-meshed netting through which a dozen or so lambs were poking their muzzles. Their mothers trotted along beside the caravan in a flock, guarded by two or three huge dogs with manes as thick as those of a lion. I say

Eyeball to Eyeball

guarded advisedly since they were constantly at risk from wolves in these highland regions, and so were the dogs whose throats were protected by collars with spikes three inches long like those worn by Cerberus in Roman times. The children either rode on the donkeys' backs or trotted beside their parents. They were a splendid cavalcade.

We watched them leave the road and look for a suitable camping site beside a stream, spread out the huge goat-hair rovers and haul them over the framework of the tent poles. It was surprising how quickly the job was accomplished and even a fire lit and coffee brewed. In the hospitable way of Nomads they invited us inside to sit on the rugs and sip from little cups.

It was at times like this that one really savoured the delights of Afghan life. Bit by bit one learned about their customs which had probably continued unchanged for many hundreds of years. But it was the way that the Nomads had so neatly fitted themselves into the agricultural economy of the country which was the most fascinating part of their story.

The Kuchi were in fact a people with a dual nationality but the distinction was an artificial one, being imposed by the British during the period of the Raj and maintained after Independence. They spent the winter in a state of hibernation in Pakistan and the summer months harvesting the crops of the Pachtu.

The centuries old pattern required was that the harvesters retained a third of the crop in lieu of a charge for their labour but they obviously could not remove the bags of grain so they sold them to some local merchant. So they practised a subsistence or barter economy and had no interest in money as such. They did on the other hand, like many eastern people, collect jewellery. Every Suk or market had a section set aside for the jewellers as we westerners do in the case of banks, building societies, insurance offices and other financial houses. It is easy to see how the practice of acquiring precious stones and treasures had arisen. A practical way of taking your wealth with you was to hang it on your person, on your hands, ears, nose, toes or round your neck and so perhaps the practice of adorning ones wife or bride arose, thereby one could combine the functions of protecting both ones wealth and loved ones at the same time. What is more, the ladies were in a better position to conceal their worldly wealth in their draperies, than under the mattress, though both had their practical advantages as hiding places.

But to appreciate the people one must, I think, know something about their history. To begin with one tends to forget that Afghanistan contains the gateway to China and the Far East, the source of so much wealth for which the European merchants would risk their all to acquire. Before the development of the art of navigation there was only one route linking east and west, later referred to as the Marco Polo Trail or Silk Route, which breached the massive barrier of the Himalayas through the Pamir Pedicle at the extreme north east corner of Afghanistan. For many centuries all the produce of the Far East, so much in demand in Europe — the tea, the silks, the china, even the opium, had to be transported many thousands of miles to the Mediterranean on the backs of camels like those used by the Kuchis.

Once inside Afghanistan the Marco Polo Route continued along the northern slopes of the Hindu Kush to the border with Iran. About half way along another road of equal importance branches off to Kabul and thence to the famous Khyber Pass and the Pakistan border. A third heads north to the romantic cities of Bokhara and Samarkand and the rest of Asiatic Russia.

Along these routes have passed the invading armies of Alexander the Great in 329 B.C.; Genghis Khan in 1227; Marco Polo in 1127 and Britain in the nineteenth century. Two major influences began to make themselves felt at this period; the expansion of the Indian and Russian empires. Britain wished to make its northern borders secure and Russia to gain access to the Indian Ocean. Inevitably the two interests conflicted, mainly in a military sense. But with the establishment of the United Nations a new emphasis was introduced. The major powers, but mainly Russia, the United States and Britain, decided to make a contribution to the development of Afghanistan in an economic sense. The Government, being very conscious of the fact that Afghanistan was lagging behind the rest of the word in this respect, welcomed any proposals which might help to remove the unbalance. The United Nations, under the auspices of the UN Technical Assistance Bureau, made a contribution to this campaign.

It coincided, not surprisingly, with the wind up of the British and other overseas Empires which had undertaken this function during the previous half century. There had been a regrettable and misleading tendency for world opinion to interpret this period as one of total exploitation which it may have been in the case of a few colonial powers but certainly not in the case of Britain. Such exploitation, as had occurred since the last war, had been at the hands of corrupt Governments in too many newly independent territories.

An incident which occurred soon after my arrival in Kabul may illustrate my point. I had decided to try and master Farsi in the evenings after work. A very pleasant retired army officer agreed to help. It was during these sessions, mentioned elsewhere, that I realised the similarities between the language and German and my teacher was most interesting on the subject.

Eyeball to Eyeball

On one occasion however he shook his head sadly and remarked how sad it was that the British never governed Afghanistan.

"But you did not give us much chance did you", I commented, "I seem to remember you wiped out one British invading force which tried to do so".

"That is true but nevertheless it was a great pity when you see how advanced Pakistan is now and how backward we are".

There was little more one could say on the subject. The general impression in fact was that little had changed in the last couple of centuries. At the same time however, due to the enormous efforts of the country people and particularly the Persian element, they had achieved or maintained a suprisingly high standard of living. But it was biblical in character.

In spring time, which of course varied enormously according to the altitude at which one happened to find oneself, the pattern of agriculture ranged from sowing in the paddy fields, as soon as the mountain peaks began to melt and flow into the irrigation trenches, to harvesting.

The farmers had adopted a wonderful control system which is probably to be found wherever irrigation is employed. It was the appointment of water bailiffs whose job was to organise a fair distribution on a rota basis between all those served by a particular "jui" as the canals were called. The bailiff was chosen democratically and well rewarded by those served by him.

The fair distribution of water was of vital importance and I shall later describe a community development scheme which was organised through the students at the Gulzar Training Centre with this objective.

The farmers had not reached the stage of using water power to drive flour mills or winnowing the grain at harvest time. Abraham would probably have felt quite at home in present-day Afghanistan. The ears of corn would be spread out on the threshing floor. Grandpa would then appear seated on a chair fixed to the threshing "chariot". This consisted of a platform weighted down by heavy rocks and the whole mounted on a bed of flints to grind up the corn. The whole apparatus was drawn by a couple of oxen, or horses or even donkeys if the family was poor, kept moving by Grandpa and his whip. Round and round they rotated converting the heads to chaff and grain. Then the young men appeared with their long handled wooden winnowing shovels, which were a combination of spade and fork. They started on the slow process of separating the grain from the chaff by chucking spadefulls of it high into the air and allowing the breeze to blow the chaff to one side, while the heavier grain fell back on to the floor, to be bagged and carted off to the homestead on the backs of donkeys.

The sight of scores of such eruptions appearing with absolute regularity against the burnished sky was a remarkable experience and reminded one of the enormous physical effort required to support life in this rugged land. The chains of donkeys loaded with bags of chaff at the end of a long day completed the cycle of rural life with the storage of fodder for livestock during the long winter months which lay ahead.

Finally one could not help being impressed by the way that Afghan men took such pleasure in fruit. On one occasion my counterpart on arrival at the training centre at Gulzar, lifted up his arms almost in a gesture of worship and remarked, "Isn't it wonderful!". I could not quite appreciate what was so wonderful. The builders rubble and materials seemed to be just as untidy and chaotic as usual and the approach road just as pot-holed.

"Yes, isn't the blossom beautiful?"

There was something incongruous about this burly man, member of a warrior race, becoming so ecstatic about the glories of spring time.

The same reaction to the beauties of the Persian garden, which a couple of men and their donkeys created in our backyard and described elsewhere was equally surprising.

It was always a pleasure to pass the stream of donkeys, their panniers piled high with red, orange and yellow fruit in the early morning on their way to market.

It was equally incongruous to find that all the schools closed down completely during the period of the Mulberry harvest. Everyone, including the teacher, were engaged in clambering about in the branches eating as much as they gathered and making themselves quite sick in the process.

And then there was the plucking of the dozen different varieties of grape, the bulk of which were dried in huge white-washed barns, honeycombed with ventilation holes and exported to Pakistan as raisins. Such was their obedience of Mohamedan law that none of this wonderful vintage was every converted to wine. It was the subject of a breach of public relations with Pakistan which will be described later.

PASHTU OR PACHTU

In our time though it is difficult to say whether the same state of affairs exist today after the Russian occupation, the Aristocrats were the Pashtu or Pathans as they were referred to by the British. The King was a Pashtu and so were his entourage. They lived in the mountains like the Highlanders in Scotland. During the Russian Invasion they were referred to as the Mujahadin. They consisted of a number of clan groups who were often at loggerheads with each other and still are. They were, like many warlike people, mainly pastoralists but they also cultivated wheat, but they had an ancient arrangement with the kuchis with regard to the harvesting of their crops which will be discussed shortly.

The Pashtu were nearly always armed and frequently involved in blood feuds. On one occasion I was driving down the new highway towards the Khyber Pass when I was stopped by a group of these warriors. They asked me politely if I would transport a colleague to hospital at Jellalabad a few miles down the road. It would hardly have been politic to refuse even though I don't normally approve of hitchhikers. Two of them piled in with the sick man who I soon found, as I had suspected, had been wounded and was not just sick. His friends told me about it as we drove on. His Uncle had shot him in revenge for some wrong committed.

CHAPTER 5

Physician Heal Thyself

BY TOM

The UN Hostel was an impressive building, constructed in the German style. There were even some antlers over the fireplace, and large sombre oil paintings in wide gilt frames hung exactly in the middle of each wall. An atmosphere of solid and somewhat ostentatious comfort prevailed. A huge mahogany radiogram, which was out of action, looked handsome at one end of the lounge.

Dr Walker emerged from the dining room at the back and walked slowly through the room to the terrace.

"I can't stand that cabbage cooked in oil" he remarked, as he lowered himself gingerly on to the hard garden seat. "None of the food seems to agree with me for that matter."

"How are you feeling today, doc?" I enquired.

"Oh, not too good, but I suppose these pills of mine will start to work sometime." He had arrived a week before to start a survey of the public health organisation of the country.

"You seem to be learning about our public health problems the hard way doc". I smiled ruefully.

"I shouldn't rely too much on your dope, though doc. In my experience, all these medicines are pretty useless. Rule number one in this country is boil all your own drinking water and don't let anyone else do it. Rule two, if you do get a go, then starve for a day or two. In due course you will get an immunity so if you survive the first six months you may live to draw your pension."

"I'm very grateful for your medical advice" he acknowledged.

Eyeball to Eyeball

I ignored the frigidity, and continued. "I always remember a very distinguished early administrator in Africa inviting me to tea at his home where he had retired in Surrey. I was amazed when the servant brought in a copper kettle and spirit stove with the tea things, and my host proceeded to boil the water and make the tea himself. He told me that he had done this every day since he first set foot in Africa forty years before, and had hardly ever had a stomach upset since. Naturally I've followed his example here, and, touch wood, I've survived pretty well.

"But you don't mean to say you do that in the hostel too?" The doctor appeared genuinely surprised that there could be any doubt about the hygienic standards of the principal international rest house in the capital.

"Of course. I invite you all to a drink tonight of whisky and home-boiled soda water. Let me warn you that anyone who touches this local stuff with the fancy label on the bottle is a maniac. I've seen the water they put into it. The only pure thing about it is the gas, but that just seems to increase the effectiveness of the poison."

"But seriously, doc" I continued, "aren't we wasting our time trying to persuade these people to adopt normal public health standards. They won't change their habits in a thousand years. All they expect is that when cholera or plague break out, as they do every few years, some kind foreigners will provide the dope to inoculate the population against them. Anyway, if we did happen to be successful in our public health schemes, this population explosion we hear so much about would become a ruddy nuclear bomb. I don't think there's much danger of that though in this country," and they all burst out laughing.

"I would like to suggest to you, Dr Walker," interposed M. Auriol with traditional French courtesy "that perhaps this poor country would be helped more if first priority was given to keeping the experts sent to advise it in good health. Would it be possible for you to - what you call it - inspect the convenience of this hostel. I believe that without doubt we are all being poisoned." "Anyway, with six of the twelve residents in bed and the rest walking-sick, as you might say, I reckon someone ought to go into the matter rather carefully, doc." The suggestion was greeted by a chorus of approval.

"I cannot go on like this" M. Auriol persisted. "There must be something wrong with this hostel. If it cannot be put right it is altogether necessary that I find a house and a cook of my own. Before I am never ill, now it is all the time."

Physician Heal Thyself

"Don't you rely too much on a cook though" I warned. "They are all the same. Self-help is the only answer." He took a sip of his coffee and wrinkled his nose in distaste as he put it back on the table, which seemed to support my case.

"Anyway, we can't complain of the weather, can we?" O'Farrell seemed determined to be cheerful, and he leant back his head to catch the warm rays of the Spring sunshine.

There was no doubt it was a beautiful spot. The daffodils had started to glow yellow in the dark grass under the poplars at the far end of the lawn. Starlings chattered in the higher branches where fresh green leaves fluttered and flashed their silvered undersides and gently floating clouds darkened the ochre crags behind.

Beyond the twelve foot wall, but unknown to them, a man was squatting unashamedly in the recess where the rubbish from the kitchen was tipped. A couple of emaciated cats were picking over the bones nearby while the flies and bluebottles which they had disturbed buzzed angrily about their ears. They need not hurry however, as the rubbish would not be removed by the donkeys of the scavenging organisation for some days yet. Although it was early Spring the sun was hot enough to make the air shimmer, and a little dust devil approached like a wraith, whirling up the leaves and paper which lay in its path and scattering them gaily to right and left.

"All right then" the doctor agreed. "Perhaps I should ask for permission to make a survey, but it seems awful cheeky to me. I find it hard to believe that this hostel could fail to be an example of how things should be done."

Aidman guffawed. "If the source of the trouble is not found soon none of us are going to be a very good advertisement of western public health methods, and you least of all, doc. Before long people will start to send me poison pen letters suggesting that the physician should heal himself before advising others what to do."

The doctor regarded him with distaste, but decided there was little point in arguing, particularly as the others appeared to share his opinion.

By the time that approval had been given for the proposed inspection, the kitchen staff had naturally had plenty of time to clean things up. As the doctor and hostel manager passed through the swing doors water still glistened on the newly sluiced floor. The cook and his helpers were wearing freshly laundered

Eyeball to Eyeball

overalls. Various large pots of meat and vegetables were simmering away on the wide stove.

"This all looks very nice and clean" remarked the doctor, hoping to establish a cordial relationship. The cook thanked him, smiling a little nervously.

"Now tell me, cook, where do you cut up the vegetables? There does not appear to be any food preparation table here."

The cook looked blankly at him, and then held a whispered conversation with his assistants, who gazed at the doctor wide-eyed.

"Surely that is not such a stupid question, is it? Where do you cut the food up?"

One of the assistants began to haul a tin tray from behind a cupboard, but was waved back by the cook, who had already decided that the best defence to this peculiar question was silence.

Walker guessed that his private information had been correct and that the assistants actually cut up the vegetables and meat squatting round the tray in the middle of the floor. No great offence this, but a little odd that the simple accepted methods of hygienic food preparation were clearly not insisted upon. In any case, the vegetables were boiled for so long that it was unlikely that any bacteria could survive, though the nutritional value of the food was probably negligible by the time it was eventually served.

"Well now, what about drinking water?" he continued genially.

The cook visibly sighed with relief. That was a question he felt he really could answer convincingly.

He led the way to a stone slab on which a number of tin containers stood, each covered by an apparently spotless cloth.

"Oh yes, that's very nice" praised the doctor, "now perhaps you could show me where you draw the water to put in them"

The cook was not to be caught out so easily. Someone had mentioned some time before that infidels liked all drinking water to be boiled. He therefore proudly produced a large copper vessel which he claimed was used for that purpose.

Physician Heal Thyself

There was nothing the doctor could do but accept this assurance, so he asked if he could be shown the water supply.

At this point Mr Jenkins the hostel manager took over and conducted the party through a smoke-blackened door and down a pitch dark passage smelling of diesel oil and the universal odour of unclean lavatories. There was a squeak as someone trod on a cat which scuttled through a hole in the wooden wall. It had apparently been waiting for its meal of scraps, or mice.

They emerged into a mid-brick hut into which a little light filtered from a small square hole high up in one wall. Most of the space was taken up by an engine which was chugging away determinedly as it pumped water up a pipe to the tank in the roof. There was a slight leak in the pipe and water was running back to mix with the oil on the floor until it eventually found its way back into the well below.

Jenkins warned the doctor to watch where he stepped as the lid over the well was a little insecure. He insisted on having a look at it, however, and a torch had to be found so that he could peer into the murky depths.

"Do you think you could find a bucket so that I can take a sample of this water?" he asked.

This took some time to find, but the operation was eventually achieved and the doctor slipped a bottle of somewhat cloudy looking liquid into his pocket. He reflected that no one probably noticed the colour of the water in this place, what with the dim lights and the amount of whisky mixed with it.

"Now, one final question" he concluded. "We passed a lavatory in the passage, didn't we? Now I wonder if you could tell me where the sewer leads to?"

"To our septic tank, doctor," Jenkins replied confidently.

"Could we see it, please?"

Walker felt that perhaps they were nearing the end of the trail, and sure enough, it was not a long one. They emerged into the bright sunshine which blinded them for a moment. The yard was small and full of crates. Steps ascended the outside wall, and it was up these that the servants presumably climbed to tip the kitchen refuse on to the rubbish heap beyond.

Eyeball to Eyeball

"The septic tank is under here" remarked the manager, pointing to a corner of the yard under a pile of empty tins.

There was obviously no hope of inspecting this today, nor had the doctor any particular desire to do so. He decided to confine himself to a few queries.

"Tell me", he began, "what is the tank lined with?"

"Why, bricks, of course."

"Burned bricks, I suppose?"

"No, sundried bricks. We have no burned bricks here."

"Cemented?"

"Oh no, just mud mortar. Like all the other buildings."

"Yes," the doctor ruminated. "And I suppose that would be about ten feet from the well over there, wouldn't you say?"

"Oh, a little more than that, I should think, perhaps fifteen feet." And he paced the distance approximately. "No, just about twelve feet. We were neither of us right, were we?" and both laughed together.

"Yes, very amusing" Dr Walker thought. "No doubt the tank and the well are interconnected, especially when it starts to rain as it did a few weeks ago."

Whether the significance of this had dawned on the manager it was difficult to say. In any case, he made no comment.

"As we obviously cannot build a new septic tank at short notice," he continued "we must take other measures, mustn't we? First of all we must obtain a water boiler and sinks and a preparation table," and the doctor reeled off a list of immediate requirements. The manager made a note of these without comment.

In due course the new equipment was obtained and installed. This was not achieved without difficulty, and various health centres had to be denuded of their furniture, since it was impossible to buy it locally. The doctor expressed himself as satisfied with the improvements made, and the staff were clearly delighted. He was a little mystified that there seemed hardly any room in the deep-freeze to keep the drinking water, as it was full of the carcases of turkeys.

Physician Heal Thyself

In view of the fact that turkey had never once appeared on the menu since his arrival, this was difficult to understand. No one thought it necessary to inform him that one of the cook's perks was to store turkeys, which he bought and slaughtered when they were cheap, and sell to foreigners at a handsome profit just before Christmas.

But the greatest disappointment occurred a week or two later when he returned to the hostel unexpectedly to collect a book he had left behind. He ran slap into the room-servant as he was filling a number of jugs and carafes of drinking water at the bathroom tap.

He had been congratulating himself that his recent recovery was due to the various public health measures which he had been instrumental in introducing.

Now he could not help wondering whether the new drug he had just received might have had something to do with it or perhaps he had developed some form of immunity.

On the other hand it might even be the electric kettle he had surreptitiously acquired. It was so difficult to know for certain.

Afghanistan must hold the record for the number of diseases it is possible to catch and the list of jabs required or recommended ran into two figures. Of course the inhabitants were not worried as they had immunity to everything by the age of six or else they expired. It is only in the case of sophisticated people like us that we become prone to anything that is going. The Americans provided the supreme example. They were so apprehensive about infections that they virtually kept themselves in moth balls. In consequence, should anything breach the barriers of prophylactics they had no natural resistance and succumbed immediately, sometimes with disastrous consequences.

Once I found myself faced with a dilemma as a result of such a situation. I frequently went on trips in the countryside with my colleagues and on one occasion we had fetched up at midday in a little town called Charikar on the Northern Highway. My friends suggested we should go to a little tea shop for something to eat and I welcomed the idea. They took me to a place with a terrace overlooking a steep gorge and a waterfall of clear water tumbling in to it. It was almost Swiss in appearance but admittedly not up to Swiss standards of hygiene. It was therefore a question of appearing stand-offish and going off by myself to eat my sandwiches in solitude or with my colleagues sharing a meal. I am afraid I chose the latter as I funked trying to explain why I regarded the food provided as potentially dangerous to my health. On the other hand it was less

Eyeball to Eyeball

difficult to avoid drinking contaminated water as one could always express a preference for tea and hence boiled and purified, since everyone seemed to prefer this. In summer most of the well known bottled soft drinks seemed to be harmless.

Anyway, by following these precautions, we seemed to avoid infections and keep free from tummy troubles. I wish we had known of the tip we were given by the Turks when we served there later - to eat natural yoghurt three times a day as they did themselves, which seemed quite fool proof.

On the occasion I started to describe earlier however, it was unfortunate that as we were settling down to enjoy our meal in its beautiful surroundings, a jeep containing, of all people, one of my UN colleagues, who was employed in the public health programme, drew up on the bridge overlooking the waterfall. He recognised me but actually refused to respond to my wave of greeting which I thought very strange. Was his eyesight failing or had he suddenly taken a dislike to me. It was neither of these things I discovered when I met him that evening.

"What on earth were you doing in that filthy dump in Charikar?" he demanded to know. "You probably have undermined all the good work we have been doing in the last six months."

"What, to try to close down all the Tea Shops in Afghanistan for their low standards of hygiene?" But it was no good.

CHAPTER 6

Gulzar

BY TOM

The Landrover finally and mercifully came to a halt at an angle of twenty degrees. That made it easier anyway to slide down off the seat and land in a patch of dry soil between two puddles. I wriggled my shoulders to get the stiffness out of them and hitched up my collar against a blast of cold air, dust and bits of paper which swept round a corner of the mudbrick building. The sun had by now topped the ridge and was starting to warm the terraced wheat fields.

A group of students was playing volleyball on a bare patch of beaten earth beside the track.

I waved to them and they greeted me cheerfully, and continued the process of getting warm. Their issue of winter clothing had not yet arrived. The negotiations between the departmental head and the contractors about the exact rake-off which the former might expect had reached a delicate stage. It was unlikely that the clothes would be ready before the first falls of snow in a month's time, and in the meanwhile, the students would have to rely on their own peasant toughness and the number of chair legs they could secrete to feed into the dormitory stove when the night winds became unbearable.

I crossed the yard and climbed the ricketty steps to the room which served as his office. Even at this time of year it was bleak, and, as usual, the stove had not yet been lit. After a few minutes however, Mahomed, the old "office-boy" edged round the creaking door, a bundle of wood shavings in one hand and a tray of glowing embers and a couple of briquettes of compressed coal dust in the other. He mumbled a good morning and placed his firemaking materials carefully beside the stove in the middle of the room.

As I sat hunched in my chair leaning against the one sound arm, I admired the old man's skill in laying the embers in a couch of shavings and then blowing them into a flame. The barrel-like bokari began to crackle as it expanded in the

Eyeball to Eyeball

heat. Smoke wriggled from odd holes and hung under the ceiling until it gradually filtered its way through the cracks at the top of the door and window. What did not escape in this manner found its way, as it was intended to do, along the metal drain pipe of a chimney which crossed the room at head height and finally passed through a hole in the outer wall.

Soon the atmosphere was warm and smoky enough for me to remove my coat, and I hung it on the stand which was one of the few pieces of office furniture provided. But in a short while the shavings had been consumed and the lumps of coal dust disappeared in acrid smoke. The few pieces of broken furniture available had been poked down the hole in the top of the stove and gone the way of all broken furniture. The temperature began to fall once more to its usual level about freezing point.

It was at this stage that a murmur of voices outside and the sad notes of a transistor gave warning of the imminent arrival of Ibrahim, the principal of the training centre. He smiled a wan greeting and it was obvious he had only struggled out of his blankets when he heard the sound of my vehicle. He placed the transistor on the desk beside him and called for tea to be brought in.

In a short while we were sipping the clear sweet liquid from little bowls which at the same time were ideal for warming the hands. By degrees Ibrahim seemed to come to life. His eyelids opened a little more with each sucking sip of tea. The time eventually came when I felt that a few remarks on administrative matters would not fall on deaf ears.

"Those stores you told me about yesterday, Ibrahim."

There was a pause as he studied the tea leaves at the bottom of the bowl.

"Oh yes, those stores, Mr Askwith"... and he relapsed into silence once more.

"Do you think we might have a look at them this morning?"

Another pause as he ruminated on this proposal.

"Why not?" he asked eventually, and called to Mahomed to fetch the storekeeper.

But it was not to be as easy as that. Nothing ever was. The storekeeper had not arrived. It was rumoured his wife was sick.

"Well, we must do it another day" I said, repeating to myself my daily prayer that I might be able to preserve an attitude of tolerant good humour combined with a spirit of firm determination. I never, as I sadly admitted to myself, managed to achieve this aim, but I put it down to a lack of practice.

"Could you tell me what is in the boxes, Ibrahim? That should help us to decide what to do with them eventually."

The Principal agreed, and called for his clerk who cringed into the room to enquire what the great man needed.

After some minutes he returned with a bundle of papers from which he extracted various lists. There were pages and pages of them. The items varied from Stanley planes to pruning knives, from blacksmith's hammers to seeds.

"There must be an enormous number of boxes" I commented.

"Yes, I believe there are." It was obvious that Ibrahim had never seen them, nor was he particularly interested in the subject.

"How long have they been here, though?"

Ibrahim studied the lists and the various stamps and signatures which appeared on them.

"It seems that they were taken over by the storekeeper, twelve, no, thirteen months ago" he calculated.

"But why have they never been used?"

Ibrahim shrugged and began to talk to his clerk to change the subject.

I ruminated over the lists which were typed on the headed paper of a well-known international organization. What on earth could they do with a hundred saws? There were not that number of students in the school and there was no such thing as a carpentry instructor. The spades would be most useful but I wondered what the students would make of the wheelbarrows. So far as he was aware such things were as yet unknown in the country.

It was some days later that the stage was reached for the ceremonial opening of the cases. It was rather like the final breaching of a prehistoric sarcophagus. The same air of tension existed. What would be found when the dust-encrusted

Eyeball to Eyeball

lids were removed? The room where they were kept was also not unlike a tomb. A vague yellow light filtered through the mud-streaked window panes, some of which had been mended with newspaper. One could dimly make out the tree trunks which supported the flat roof. A little more light was coming through a hole in one corner where the wickerwork had rotted away and allowed the mud ceiling to collapse. Heavy boxes lay about the earth floor, their markings almost obliterated by the mud which had poured down when the last snow melted and leaked through the cracks in the roof.

The great occasion marked the culmination of days of effort. First the labourers had been unable to help because they were needed for an emergency job on the farm. Then the students had had to be measured for their overcoats on the day fixed for the task. Then Ibrahim said that boarding should be obtained and shelves put up for the tools, but he failed to obtain permission to buy it, and anyway, it would have taken weeks to construct them.

So finally, everyone agreed that the students should open the boxes and unpack the tools, and the lids of the boxes would be used as temporary shelves. Everyone stood around in the half-light and waited for Abid the storekeeper who had found a crowbar to prise open the first case.

A cloud of dust swirled up and the rusted nails screeched as the lid was wrenched off. A layer of shavings was removed and then half a dozen students began to extricate the tools from their stained wrappings. It was like Christmas morning. Everyone, for no real reason, started to get excited about what Santa Claus had brought. The students crowded round chattering and ejaculating as the various strange implements emerged.

First there was a collection of spokeshaves, implements hitherto unknown in the country. Then a number of superb chisels appeared, or perhaps it would be more correct to say that they had been superb once. Now they looked as if they had caught some revolting skin disease.

As box after box was emptied the cries of bewilderment increased. Carpentry tools in local use were confined to about half a dozen simple and robust implements. The most popular one was the adze which could be used for trimming roof timbers or sharpening a pencil. Holes were drilled with a peculiar instrument which resembled the bow of a violin, the string being wound round the bit to spin it. Crude implements, perhaps, but quite effective for the rough carpentry which was all that anyone required. Apart from that, there was little to go wrong, and if they did break they were not too difficult to repair.

I gazed with mounting horror at the growing piles of expensive equipment. It was not merely the criminal waste of leaving it to rust and disintegrate that appalled me but the incredible folly of providing tools for which, when they broke, as they inevitably would, there would be no replacements or means of repairing them.

"Who on earth ordered this stuff, Ibrahim?" I blurted out in exasperation, and regretted immediately that I had not kept a guard on my tongue.

Ibrahim was obviously hurt.

"We didn't ask for it, sir. It was that technical assistance man who was out here a couple of years ago who decided we needed it."

"Yes, of course, I didn't mean to criticise you. What I really meant was what was it ordered for?"

"Oh, I don't know, sir. Perhaps some of it is for making demonstrations in the projects."

A flood of questions were pressing for an answer but I resisted the temptation to ask them. It was all so futile. Neither Ibrahim nor anyone else would have the answer or, for that matter, would care. They hadn't asked for the tools, their government hadn't even paid for them. They just represented extra work for someone which no one in his right mind would go in search of.

As the boxes were emptied they were turned over to make tables or shelves and the tools were grouped together on top. They would all have to be cleaned. That meant that sand must be found, for sandpaper was unknown. Then I noticed a pile of stuff emerging from a box, but it was clear that it was all stuck together and already crumbling. To relieve my exasperation I turned from the scene.

"Let's go and look at the other store rooms and decide where to put it all, Ibrahim. We don't want it all to get muddled up. "

We moved from one dark and dusty room to another. One would do for the agricultural equipment, another for the seeds and fertilizer, a third for the blacksmith's tools.

"Where shall we put the carpentry tools? What about this room in here, Ibrahim?" and I pointed to a locked door at the end of a passage.

Eyeball to Eyeball

"Oh, that is full, sir."

"What of?"

"That equipment made by Mr Clay. I told you about it."

I remembered now. This fellow had been employed by one of the aid missions. He was a highly resourceful and skilled individual. He had been engaged to develop ways and means of manufacturing tools and implements from materials available in the country. He had made water pumps, mechanical seeders, even primitive washing machines, and the store was full of his inventions.

I had always been at a loss to understand why these tools had never been manufactured locally on a wide scale. They were, it was admitted, just what were needed. It was not for some months and after Ibrahim had grown to trust me that he admitted that the government considered that the implements were too primitive. What they wanted was modern equipment such as was in use in more advanced countries. If it broke, then the foreigners must arrange for replacements. Was not this the purpose of technical assistance? The idea of developing local skills to provide for local needs was a new and strange one. Even though Afghans had for centuries been past-masters in improvisation. Eventually Mr Clay left, a disappointed man, his mission unfulfilled.

I suddenly wondered whether this was the reason why all these expensive modern implements had been bought? But if so, why had they never been used? Why had they been left to decay in this dreary catacomb?

During the following weeks the tools were gradually sorted out and cleaned up. Ibrahim always seemed to be resentful of this activity. He used to stand at the door, and if he had had his way he would have searched each student as he left to make sure that he was not secreting some sledge hammer or shovel about his person. At last, everything was in a reasonable state of order. About three quarters of the tools were now serviceable. The rest were beyond redemption. The promised shelves had of course not materialized, but the cracks in the roof had been plastered with fresh cow dung and straw so, with any luck, the spring rain would not penetrate.

I walked round with Ibrahim and Abid to review the situation. It was rather like a kit inspection with gear laid out on box lids all over the floor.

"The next question, Ibrahim" I remarked "is again, what do we do with the stuff?"

Ibrahim ruminated once more over this original query. It was, however, too much for him.

"What do you mean, sir, do with it?"

I took a firm hold of myself.

"Well, how are we going to make use of it all?"

"Oh, I see, of course." It had at last become clear to Ibrahim that something further must be done, however distasteful and awkward that might be.

"First of all, I suggest that we put the tools we need at the centre into circulation. We could start a carpentry class. We can teach the students how to prune fruit trees properly, and perhaps even do some simple plumbing, so that when a pump needs a new washer it doesn't have to stand idle until someone comes out from the capital in a few months time."

"That would be a good idea" Ibrahim agreed, but obviously with little enthusiasm.

"We have, of course, got no carpentry instructor", he remarked as an afterthought.

It occurred to me that perhaps I might do the job myself. I hadn't really done any carpentry since I was at school, but I did know how to replace a washer. That would mean that apart from my weekly English class I would be giving instruction in Local Government, techniques of persuading village people to accept new ideas, visual aids, village organization, and two or three other subjects including games, and now carpentry. It seemed to suit all concerned in any case. The more classes I took the less the other members of the staff had to do, also the fewer staff the government had to engage. The students themselves always seemed to appreciate them too. They said that they were so much more interesting than being read to from a text book which they, and more often than not the teacher himself, did not understand.

"But what about the rest of it. There is obviously about three times as much as we need in the centre."

Eyeball to Eyeball

"Yes" Ibrahim agreed. "I expect the rest is intended for the instructors who are now working in the villages."

"I suppose you will be getting it sent out to them in due course then." Which comment elicited a grunt which might or might not have implied agreement.

So the carpentry classes got under way but only on one condition; each time the necessary tools had to be drawn from the store and signed for by me. At the end of the class they had to be collected and returned in the same way. Presumably if one of the students did secrete a saw up his trouser leg I would be held responsible for its loss. Anyway, so far they seemed to be playing fair. In fact, they were so delighted to learn carpentry that the class leader had taken on the duty of checking the tools. He was a ferocious young man with black hair and I trembled to think what would happen if a student failed to hand in his issue of tools correctly.

But the problem of the balance of the tools remained unsolved. They continued to slumber in their rows in the semi darkness, and no doubt wondered why they had been taken so far from home, where people appreciated and cherished them, to this distant land where apparently no one cared how beautiful or valuable they were. Months, in fact, passed until the whole affair became too much for me. I went to see the head of the department, but nothing resulted so I went to see the local chief of the organization which had supplied the equipment in the first place.

It all seemed to have been fruitless until one day when I went into the store to collect some equipment I found it had all disappeared.

"So at last it's out being used for what it was intended, Ibrahim" I remarked cheerfully.

Ibrahim smiled. "Yes, I hope so."

"What do you mean you hope so? Why shouldn't it be used? This is what these former students are always telling us they need - implements to demonstrate better methods of farming, and so on."

There was a pause as Ibrahim obviously wondered whether to confide in me. He always did that, but did not shed much light on the subject. As a result, I was usually compelled to read between the lines and to guess the reasons for some incomprehensible state of affairs. On this occasion Ibrahim apparently felt that there was no harm in letting me into the secret, or perhaps that if he failed to do so I might become exasperated and persistent, and this was always so trying.

"I see you don't know about our system of storekeeping" he began.

"That's certainly true, but I'm learning fast. I have to sign my name and take responsibility if someone else loses something belonging to the centre almost every day."

"No, that is something else," Ibrahim continued soothingly, "in my country the post of storekeeper is quite well paid compared to many jobs. It is also a very quiet job. But if you want to be a storekeeper you have to pay a large deposit to the government. If anything gets lost from your store, then you have to pay for it from your deposit. So it is much easier to keep it locked up all the time. In fact, the storekeeper, Abid, only lets you have the tools for your carpentry class because I told him you are a rich foreigner and would be able to pay for anything which got lost. As far as the equipment which has been sent out to the Projects is concerned that will by now have been locked up again in their stores."

"So you mean it will not after all have been used for demonstration purposes?" I asked in bewilderment.

"I very much doubt it." Ibrahim replied equably.

CHAPTER 7

Foreigners

BY TOM

We had to accept right from the start that we were foreigners and that we had to adjust our lifestyle to that of the many communities which inhabited this polyglot of a country. And what a mixture we were!

At the time I suppose the largest foreign contingent was that of the Americans followed by the Russians, although no one really knew how many there were. The British, having been such a dominating influence in the area for centuries were now a comparatively small minority. We only discovered somewhat later that there was a sizeable German settlement also. They kept very much to themselves and so were the subject of some speculation. Finally there were our colleagues in the United Nations Mission who came from every corner of the globe, a high proportion being British, the perennial Nomads, and as one would expect people of Asiatic origin, situated as we were next to the Indian Sub Continent.

Not unnaturally, each group tended to keep themselves to themselves but the UN mission seemed to occupy a central role and mix with everyone.

The Diplomatic Corps tended to keep its relationships mainly on the official plane. Even the cocktail parties which they attended nightly and often more frequently were a means of exchanging information of a less confidential nature between themselves. But it must have been exhausting and could have been bad for the liver. I remember on one occasion our military attaché flopping into a chair in our flat and gasping "I'm awash with squash" on the last of his nightly round of cocktail parties. I imagined that for anyone who valued his health it was the only safeguard.

I suppose it was the same in all the capitals of the world. Most countries, particularly since the 1960s had their Independence Days which were naturally the occasion of a party financed by the Ambassadors or Ministers from their entertainment accounts. The British in particular who had been the principal

Eyeball to Eyeball

colonial powers, but also the French, must have been responsible for much of the alcoholic suffering in overseas embassies. The parties were also the source of many an unguarded revelation and one of the qualities of a good diplomat was his ability to hold his liquor as well as reserve his discretion.

One of the agreeable sides of working with the United Nations was the opportunity it gave one of getting to know nationals of other countries. The two Russian members of our team were particularly agreeable characters, one of whom was the interpreter as I have already mentioned. On one occasion he came round for a drink at our house and he noticed our old portable windup gramophone and pile of records. Martinoff, the English-speaking one as we might call him, asked if he might look through them as we were all starved of such luxuries as records and books since, of course, radio reception in that mountainous country was atrocious.

"Ah" cried Martinoff "A Victor Silvestor! My favourite."

"Good. Let's put it on."

It happened to be a record brought out by one of the boys during the last holidays. Actually I couldn't stand the thing.

When it was finished, Martinoff expressed his delight. I rather think he was being polite. At any rate I sensed our opportunity of getting rid of the thing so as he was leaving I pressed it into his hands. He was obviously embarrassed but that made the situation all the more droll.

To my surprise there was a knock on our door next morning and Martinoff appeared, the perfect diplomat, as he probably was, disguised as a UN expert, and probably a member of the KGB. One always suspected that by persuading the UN to accept an interpreter, at Russian expense of course, they killed two birds with one stone. As well as qualifying for an additional expert, the Russians guarded themselves against possible defection or betrayal in some way. Perhaps one was just being fanciful however, which is liable to happen when working on the borders of the Soviet Union in a country divided by an Iron Curtain, even though it might be more metaphysical than real.

However, to continue the tale, Martinoff, always the diplomat, said how much he had enjoyed the evening with us and would we accept a small gift - an LP Chaliapin, as an expression of their appreciation. I felt that we had ended up on the credit side which was what was intended. It would not do for the great Soviet Union to feel under an obligation to even so insignificant a citizen of

Foreigners

Britain, masquerading as a United Nations Official as myself. Honour, with her tongue in cheek, had been satisfied.

We got to know each other much better as time went on, until on the eve of our departure for England, we once more decided to have a farewell lunch together. For some reason I remember it very clearly, for we were enjoying a meal of roll mop herring acquired at some UN Commisariat, washed down with some genuine Russian Vodka provided I suppose by the equivalent commintern emporium.

In the course of our festivities, Martinoff admired Patricia's typing of some reports she had done for me, for competent typists were at a premium in Kabul as one might expect. He continued by wondering whether she would be prepared to sell him her machine when we left. I was a little surprised because one got the impressions that all such luxuries were readily available to the Russians and if not, they would be reluctant to admit the fact. Presumably this was not the case they were allowed to acquire second hand but not new goods from overseas. Anyway she had no objection to doing a deal and updating her somewhat ancient machine when we got back to England, and we sealed it with another glass of Vodka and the last of the roll mop herrings.

But I was a little amused by his English. Apparently the Foreign Office or whatever it may be called in Moscow had set up a language school for budding diplomats. Martinoffs teacher had obviously spent some years in England after the first world war because his colloquialisms were full of Bertie Wooster expressions like "top ho" and "spiffing". One couldn't help feeling that his instructors could do with a bit of updating but of course putting up an "iron curtain" was not the best way of achieving this.

Soon after my arrival in Kabul I decided to take lessons in Farsi from an Afghan colleague.

As we sipped our whisky, which I noted did not appear to be contrary to his particular form of Muslim faith, he sadly shook his head.

"It is a great pity that you British did not rule us like you did in Pakistan" he observed.

"Why ever do you say that? You spent your whole life fighting us and in fact slaughtered the whole garrison on one occasion."

Eyeball to Eyeball

"Yes that is true I agree, but that is the reason that we are so far behind our blood brothers who live across the border. We have no railways and until the Americans came, no roads or good schools."

And that of course is still the same today.

The Americans are a very different community. We had much more in common with them and they in turn had greater sympathy with the Afghan for some reason. But they had a horror and fear of their low standard of living and ideas of hygiene. As a result they lived in houses which were identical with those they had inhabited in the States, and were provided with food and even water like that "back home". As a result they were very prone to any local diseases which happened to be prevalent should they ever emerge from their hygienic cocoons. But worst of all they suffered from "culture shock" in a big way and a number of books have been written on this subject. As a result they were provided with the same social activities they were accustomed to in the States.

One of these was the KADS - "The Kabul Amateur Dramatic Society". Possibly as a result of a friendship with our very dear friends, the Cohens, who was engaged in a large educational project financed by Columbia University I got involved in their productions. I never quite understood why until Munro confided that they were looking for a Britisher who could take on board some of their Blimp British parts. What they had in mind was I think the English character in St Joan. George Bernard Shaw was a great favourite with the KADS. I suppose possibly because he was so "anti" British. I was the most Blimpish Britisher around at the time who was prepared to stand up and get a laugh.

Anyway I did my best which was not very good for I had great difficulty in learning my part. But it was great fun and took ones mind off many of the frustrations which beset ones life.

Another form of recreation was skiing. One would have thought that in a country like Afghanistan someone might have thought of introducing skiing, but it was not exactly a country with tourist potential. But there were a number of foreigners who thought the opportunities were being neglected and decided to construct a ski-lift themselves. I had never done any skiing myself but was persuaded to try. The run itself was no longer than 500 meters and consisted of an overhead cable, a diesel engine picked up in some *suk* (like everything else one might require) and a windlass. We took it in turns to supply the fuel and take charge of the plant. A friend kindly bought me some boots on his leave in Austria and to give me some instructions in the gentle art of avoiding breaking

Foreigners

a leg with the nearest suitable hospital three thousand miles away, and we were off. It was most exhilarating but I decided that I had left it a bit late to start at the age of 50.

What I was anxious to do was to indulge in my lifetime hobby of painting, but here again I found myself somewhat frustrated. At weekends, that is to say on Fridays, I used to drive out to what appeared to be a suitable vantage point and get to work. Almost inevitably, a soldier with a rifle poked his head above a nearby ridge and began waving his arms at me. I thought he was just being friendly and waved back, which made him even more agitated and he began running towards me.

Although I knew little farsi at the time, I knew enough to realise that for some reason I was not welcome in that particular locality. So in some disappointment I began to pack up my gear and return to the car.

On my return to Kabul, I asked my colleagues what they thought I had done wrong.

"Oh I expect he thought you were a spy, Tom."

"But there was nothing to spy on except a magnificent view of the Hindu Kush a hundred miles away, with some camels and the odd farm in the foreground" I complained.

"But that was quite enough. Didn't you know that in Victorian times, all army officers were expected to learn to sketch so that they could provide their cartographers with impressions of the countryside in the event that patrols might be required in the area."

Light began to dawn. That would explain why the army arranged regular Art Exhibitions, not to develop latent artistic talents, but sketches of the terrain likely to be of value in future campaigns. The Afghans had obviously got wise to this and logically linked artistic potential or otherwise with espionage.

Thus to my disappointment was my harmless pastime frustrated and the world denied the opportunity of enjoying some masterpieces of Afghan scenery.

We were lucky to have the opportunity of swimming however. The bath was situated at the International Club and was usually crowded in the summer. We noticed that most of the bathers were congregated at the far end of the pool, but to our surprise they all turned out to be Germans. It took time for the penny to

Eyeball to Eyeball

drop. They could only be refugees from Germany and they were certainly not Jews. Perhaps they were returning to their spiritual home - the country of the Aryans and possibly the language was not all that dissimilar either.

They apparently kept a low profile but occasionally indulged in a party. If this should lead to a fracas among themselves, the police might be called in and the guilty parties lodged in gaol for a period. Since food was not provided in Afghan gaols, their relatives were kept busy keeping them alive.

It was only later that I remembered that when I was applying for a temporary membership of the Peshawas Club, I was told that they did not reciprocate with the International Club. It was not really very surprising.

We were in Afghanistan a little before the Hippy Trail became a feature of the Middle East. Who would have expected that the last followers of Alexander's armies would similarly be European although not in this instance in search of plunder unless narcotics can be classed as such. Neither were they armed, but ostensibly in search of peace and spiritual relaxation which was so difficult to find in the sophisticated and materialistic culture of their homeland. Some of my children's friends who called in on their way to India seemed to be greatly enjoying themselves. Nowadays the Hippy Trail has largely been abandoned in favour of the Gap Year - or the Gap Two Year according to taste. In our time there were also VSO's or Peace Corps. Whatever they called themselves, the idea was the same. They were satisfying the natural whim of young people to explore another part of the world before settling down to commuting or rearing babies - or both.

Perhaps the strangest community of all however was that of the British Embassy Staff. The building itself was a brilliant pile of columns and white plaster surrounded by lawns and shrubberys and watered by sprinklers like any Sunningdale mansion. It had one of the finest libraries of Afghan history outside London and had every facility that members of a Country Club would expect.

It was however the last of a series of Embassies to be erected following the sacking of its predecessor. As such its inhabitants seemed to suffer from a kind of siege mentality. Walled in on the outskirts of the town with Embassy Guards at the gate they were not unnaturally apprehensive of what the local populace might do to them.

It was however surprising at the time that a young couple we met and invited to drinks at our humble Afghan house in Shari Nau were so impressed with the atmosphere and friendliness of our neighbours that they asked for and were

Foreigners

reluctantly given permission to live outside the Embassy Compound. They seemed completely happy slumming in the city and told us that they no longer felt immured in the Embassy. What was probably of more importance, their Afghan friends did not feel inhibited by the Lodge Guards when they wanted to make a friendly call.

CHAPTER 8

Cautionary Tales

BY TOM

A. V.I.P.s

There was an unusual atmosphere of activity that morning. The Principal was, for instance, out of bed by half past eight, and already on his way down to the training centre by nine. He had not even had time to shave or to tell me what it was all about. Shortly afterwards, the students began to emerge from the side entrance, each carrying a shovel or a pick or pushing a wheelbarrow. They streamed down the track which connected the Centre with the main road a mile away, yelling to each other and happy to be out of the classroom for the day. I strolled down and joined the last of the procession.

"What is going on, Mahommed?" I asked one of the staff who was accompanying them.

"We have just been told that a visitor is coming, and the road has to be made up."

"He must be a very important visitor then. Who is he?"

"I don't know, sir. They didn't tell us."

That is lie number one, I thought, but I suppose there must be some reason for the secrecy.

Even the Principal, whom I met on his way back to the Centre, professed ignorance of the identity of the visitor.

"Will you excuse me, sir," he said, "I must go and see that the guest house is ready as we have to arrange lunch there tomorrow."

Eyeball to Eyeball

The guest house had been built a few years earlier so that a certain Head of State might have somewhere to drink a cup of tea in the course of a tour of the area. It was more than a simple tea house, however, and was more like a small suburban two-storeyed villa. It was said to have been built in six weeks, which compared well with the Training Centre which had been under construction for four years, and only the dormitories had so far been completed and even so condemned, as I have mentioned.

Next day, the frantic preparations continued. All the dormitories had to be cleaned, the broken chairs removed from the classrooms, and the library dusted. It was only on such occasions that it was, in fact, opened. At other times it was like a shrine, and the door was kept perpetually closed. It was full of books provided by various international organisations and well wishers, which were kept carefully locked away in glass cases. The new projector had been brought out of its case so that at any rate it might be on display. Everyone hoped that the visitor would not ask to see some transparencies, for the thing had not worked for months. The bulb had burned out and no one had thought it worthwhile replacing it. The slides themselves were of other countries, and when not incomprehensible were unsuitable for instructional purposes.

In one way, the fact that the Centre was still under construction was an advantage. Visitors could be shown the impressive foundations, and be asked to imagine the splendours to come. The fact that the building had been under construction for many years and no one knew how long it would take to complete need never be mentioned. Many of the delays, in fact, were due to the need to agree on a price with the contractor before he started up again each year in the spring. Actually, the more it cost the better it suited everyone, for this meant a larger share for the very interested officials.

Next morning, a somewhat harassed Principal walked down what would eventually become a precinct with shrubs and possibly a fountain. It was now a pile of rubble which was almost impassable in wet weather.

"Everything under control, Ibrahim?" I asked solicitously.

"I think so, sir." He seemed to think he was being made fun of. "It is very important that everything should be in order."

"Of course, Ibrahim, but who is our visitor?"

"He is the Chairman of a Committee of the United Nations, I believe."

Cautionary Tales

I managed to conceal a smile, and Ibrahim carefully avoided meeting my eye. We both understood, though neither admitted this to the other, the reason for all the fuss. The government was clearly anxious to maintain the illusion of progress, at any rate until the departure of the honoured guest.

A cloud of dust in the distance gave warning of the approaching procession of vehicles. They drove up, and were greeted by a line of clapping students. Those whose uniforms had not yet arrived had been concealed in the dormitories.

The party made its way through the gardens to the guest house. It was set in a beautiful position. Banks of potted plants had been arranged on wooden stands near the entrance. They had been brought out from the greenhouse, which, rumour had it, was maintained solely to provide plants for favoured government officials. All around towered the mountains. The slopes of the foothills were painted with every shade of red and brown which gave way higher up to the steel and indigo of the rocks. The more distant hills lay mauve or blue where the drifting clouds cast their shadows across them. Remote and snowy ranges could be glimpsed beyond the passes.

We climbed up to the sitting room on the first floor where an even better view was obtainable. The guest of honour was seated on the sofa next to the senior government man present. The other officials were arranged in order of seniority on either side. I found a seat somewhat farther away.

Arnold Hunter from the United Nations was a New Zealander. He was grey-haired and hollow-chested and had obviously had an exhausting morning. The Minister sat forward on the sofa, his fat legs spread wide, and attended to his guest, offering him cigarettes, sweets and nuts, all of which he declined. Fruit was called for, and plates of juicy apricots, peaches and plums were handed round.

When he judged that the visitor was sufficiently refreshed, he asked the Principal to tell him about the Training Centre and its activities.

"Well, Mr Hunter," he began, planting his podgy knuckles on his knees. "I hope you were pleased with our little tour."

Hunter assured him he had enjoyed it very much, and then with almost a wink at me added, "we certainly saw plenty of girls' schools, and that women's class was most impressive. How many of them have you got?"

Eyeball to Eyeball

"Of course, you must remember that we are only at the beginning of our programme, sir, but we hope to extend it right through the country in due course," the Minister explained.

Very smooth, I applauded silently, but you failed to mention that foreign advisers have been working here for the last five years, and have not yet got beyond the first women's group. You'll have to speed up if you want to cover the country this century. But it's a nice place to take visitors to and show them how emancipated the government really is.

Hunter addressed me directly.

"You have been working here for the last year, what are your impressions about the way things are progressing?" he asked.

"Oh, things are improving all the time," I said, but before I could get any further, the Minister was saying that time was short, and they would have to start their tour of the school's centre. Again, I had the impression that Hunter winked invisibly. The Minister was obviously apprehensive that he might not be receiving the glowing picture that he deserved. It was hardly enough to say things were improving, when the government denied the fact that there was anything wrong.

The tour of the Centre started. I could not help admiring the way Ibrahim had mapped out a route which would successfully by-pass the black spots. They avoided entering by the door next to the blocked-up drains for instance and did not inspect the dormitory where the sick were. No one wanted awkward questions to be asked about why they had not been taken to hospital. They looked at the classroom which had the blackboard and the chalk and a complete set of chairs. They missed out the dining room altogether, as for lack of benches, the students had to feed standing round a table.

The visitor was shown the new classrooms under construction. The workmen had plastered up the cracks in the ceilings the day before, and only an expert could notice that the building was actually structurally unsound. Insufficient cement had gone into the concrete, for the contractor had been hard pressed to cover his expenses after providing for handouts to various officials.

The tour of inspection went off quite well, all things considered. After all, everyone was by now quite experienced in conducting such operations. It was unfortunate that the visitor had chosen Ali's exercise book to have a look at. After all, he was one of the few who was actually illiterate. No one knew exactly

Cautionary Tales

why he had been accepted for the course, but it was surmised that one of the senior members of the department had given instruction that he should be enrolled. It appeared that his father was a man of some wealth and influence, and it was hardly his fault that his son happened to be mentally retarded.

It was also a little mystifying why Mr Hunter had asked what age village leaders should be to cut much ice with the traditional village elders. No one but he had noticed that one of the fourteen year old students, who had also gained acceptance on the course in some inexplicable way, had slipped into the back of the classroom although he had been sent on an errand that afternoon. There did not seem much, in fact, that had missed the New Zealander's eagle eye.

At any rate he did seem to have been impressed by the slide projector, though he had asked whether pictures of successful schemes in the project areas had been taken for instructional purposes. Raschid felt that he had got round this question rather neatly by agreeing that this was an excellent idea, and suggesting to Ibrahim that he should act on it immediately. Luckily Mr Hunter did not ask if there had actually been any successful schemes since the campaign was launched ten years previously.

Having completed the somewhat hasty tour of the Centre, the party clambered into the cars once more for another dusty drive to the model village. Of course, it was not called a model village. The fiction was preserved that it was typical of all villages. But it was conveniently situated just outside the capital where foreigners might be taken for an afternoon drive between conference sittings.

Though not invited I tacked on at the tail, and followed the billowing dust clouds of the official cavalcade. I let them get away a bit so as not to have to breathe the dust, and when I arrived I found them drawn up at the entrance to the village where Mr Hunter was being introduced to the village elders. These old men were trotted out, much against their will, every time a visitor was brought there. They were always introduced as the Village Development Committee. This sounded very progressive, and democratic, and who was to know that they were usually only assembled when the government, in the shape of the headman, wished to give them any instructions. I remembered how impressed the Head of State referred to earlier had been with the spirit of this village. Everyone had been furiously working on paving the road with stone which was being brought by strings of donkeys. It was fortunate that the eminent stranger was ignorant of the language, or he would have been shocked at the muttered curses of the villagers at being forced to do this work at harvest time.

Eyeball to Eyeball

The village elders followed the official party as it picked its way to the model house, or to be more exact, one of the model houses, as visitors were never shown the others, which were empty. They had in fact never been occupied, as the design was quite unsuitable for the domestic needs of the villagers. The show house was occupied by the midwife, at any rate on the occasion of ceremonial visits such as this. At other times she lived with her husband in the capital.

She greeted Mr Hunter and the other visitors with the ease and sophistication of a woman educated in Europe, which in fact she was.

Mr Hunter was pleased to see the immaculate UNICEF equipment, the baby scales, the couch, and the rest of the paraphenalia. It struck him as being perhaps a little too immaculate for things which were allegedly in daily use, but that was by the way. He was at any rate most impressed by the neat girl in her white uniform and high-heeled shoes, who, with complete aplomb, showed off the clinic as if this was a regular occurrence, as indeed it was.

Raschid beamed with satisfaction as he later ushered his guest into the Reading Room where tea had been prepared. He felt confident that his mission had been fulfilled, and that the Prime Minister would be satisfied with his efforts. Mr Hunter could not fail to give a good report to his committee about the country's social policy. It had been a well-conducted tour, and there had been no breakdowns in the customary itinerary. Good Muslim or not, he would enjoy the whisky that his friend Mr Alvarez had obtained for him this evening.

Mr Hunter, though for somewhat different reasons, was thankful that the ordeal by propaganda was nearly at an end. Why, he wondered, did these governments imagine that such people as he relied on conducted tours for their information. There were so many more reliable ways than that to obtain the required facts.

As they emerged to rejoin their vehicles on the last leg of the tour, a woman shrouded in the traditional tent-like veil crossed the road, and slipped into the back of one of the cars. Hunter with difficulty stifled a whistle of astonishment. He could never mistake those neat, white high-heeled shoes which flashed for a moment beneath her draperies.

Sophistication, it would seem, was strictly and only for foreign eyes, and privileged ones at that.

B. I WISH TO SERVE MY COUNTRY

"This matter of your counterpart, Mr Askwith, which we discussed the other day" Jelib remarked to open the conversation once the tea had arrived. "I have a young man who, I think, will suit you very well."

I thanked him, but without marked enthusiasm. "Is a young man what is really needed though?" I asked. "I thought the idea was that I should train someone fairly senior who would be responsible for policy."

"Yes" Jelib agreed, "but you see, the difficulty is that the senior men do not usually know English and they are also, between you and me, a bit conservative. So if you had a younger man as your counterpart, he would learn from you more quickly and be more effective in the long run."

There was obviously nothing more to be said, and in due course, a young man made his appearance in my office and told me he had been sent by the Director to discuss the question of a counterpart.

I assumed that the Director very properly wished me to assure myself that the candidate would be suitable, so I began to question him about his background.

It seemed that Hassan was well educated and must therefore also be well-connected. I was a little mystified by the fact that he had apparently attended the Faculty of Internal Affairs at the University, which did not appear to have much connection with his future role in connection with community development.

"Well, I am very interested in community development, Mr Askwith," Hassan explained. "I feel it is a very important thing for my country."

I was becoming rather impressed by the young man. (He obviously had the right ideas.) There were not many who had such a farsighted judgment of the real needs of the country. I felt I must get to the bottom of this business of the agricultural degree however, and questioned him further about it.

"But I did not want to study agriculture Mr Askwith, I was just told to".

I had indeed been told that this happened all too frequently. It did seem a little strange however that Hassan should be suggested as a local government officer when there was such a crying need for agriculturalists.

Eyeball to Eyeball

I continued to draw out information about the young man and gained a very favourable impression of his intelligence and keenness. I said as much, and Hassan seemed suitably flattered.

"Yes, Mr Askwith, I am very anxious to serve my country. You see we have much to learn from other countries and we can only do this if we educated people get more knowledge of the latest methods of government. I hear that your country, Mr Askwith, is very advanced in local government."

I agreed with appropriate modesty that I believed this was so. At the end of the discussion, however, I was a little taken aback by Hassan enquiring whether he would be awarded an overseas fellowship at the conclusion of his apprenticeship. Hassan pointed out that he had already been offered a fellowship by another country as a matter of fact, though, of course, he had not yet accepted it. This sounded to me awfully like blackmail, and it suddenly occurred to me that instead of it being me who was assessing Hassan's suitability for the post, I myself was being interrogated by the young man with regard to its ultimate attractions.

I was so taken off guard that I said I would have to make enquiries about this, and would let him know later.

That evening as usual, the unmarried or unaccompanied Advisers who lived in the hostel were sitting round the oil stove in the lounge. The thing bubbled noisily from time to time as it drew on more of the smelly fuel. A draught of frozen air found its way in from the snow-bound world outside in spite of the thick curtains which covered the windows.

The four men met together each evening and looked forward to this opportunity of expressing some of the exasperation which they had had to bottle up during the day. The whisky relaxed the tensions and loosened the tongues. I often wondered how much of the outspoken comments which were exchanged found their way back to the government by way of the steward, who always seemed to be lurking behind the curtains. No one particularly cared if they did, however, and in some ways hoped they would.

I mentioned the business of Hassan that afternoon.

"Naturally he wanted to be certain there was to be a fellowship at the end," I remarked. "You don't imagine he would agree to waste a year with you unless there was something to make it worth while."

Cautionary Tales

"Why are you always so bloody cynical, Askwith?" O'Farrell answered angrily. "I thought he was a very decent chap - all things considered", he added, remembering the slight sense of disillusionment he had felt at the end of the otherwise very agreeable conversation.

O'Farrell snorted "Come off it, and anyway, you're damned lucky he does want a fellowship. That's about the only way you will be able to get any work out of him. Keep it dangling in front of his nose as long as possible, though, once it's all fixed up, he'll just cock a snook at you."

"And another thing" O'Farrell continued, "think yourself lucky that you have been offered a counterpart at all. If you hadn't been, how do you think you could do a damn thing? Without knowing the language, how could you even begin?"

I had to admit to myself that this made some sense. "But surely", I continued, "the whole point of these assignments is that one passes on one's knowledge to the nationals?"

O'Farrell choked, and dabbed his coat where the whisky had spilled.

"That's one of them" he admitted and winked to the older hands. "But look at old Amin. His counterpart disappeared one day and has never been seen since. For some reason the government wished his continued contact with the field severed and what better way than cutting out his tongue. Could his ideas have been too forward looking, do you think? Now he just sits in his office, trying to think what he will put in his next quarterly report to headquarters. Luckily he has a fertile imagination. No, I'm not exaggerating. This is fact, so do come down to earth. It's either that, or go up the wall."

Eyeball to Eyeball

C. LOCAL COMMENTS

Hassan and his friends had not the advantage of duty-free whisky to beguile their evenings, but a variety of sickly bottled drinks provided an alternative. They squatted together on the thick carpet snug in the warmth of the iron stove which stood beside it.

"Did our new Adviser believe your story that you had been offered the other fellowship?" Ahmed enquired, after Hassan had described his efforts of the afternoon.

"I don't know, but he swallowed the bit about my wanting to study local government."

They all sniggered.

"And what does your uncle, the Minister, think about local government, Hassan? Does he like the idea of such socialist systems in our country?"

No one thought it necessary to comment.

"I hear that Jelib is very keen on your working in his department, Hassan. It is difficult enough to get any educated people to go into such a dead-end outfit. He's bound to help you get a fellowship if you want it, just to keep you there."

"I think you are stupid to try and get a fellowship to England, Hassan. You ought to try for an American one. They give you much better allowances."

"That may be true, but they say it is more expensive there."

"Not if you ask to stay with a family. All you have to do is to say you want to get to know the American way of life."

"There might even be a pretty daughter too. They don't mind you taking them out alone there."

"When I went on my travelling fellowship, I stayed in rest houses very cheaply. After six months I had almost saved enough to buy a car."

"That may be, but it's better to get a degree. Then you can get a better job when you come back. Some of the Colleges are very kind. Even if you haven't done any work they say you are a poor foreigner and can't understand properly, and let you pass."

"It's all right for Hassan. It doesn't matter if he has a degree or not with a father in the Cabinet."

"Maybe, but how long will the Government last? If it gets thrown out I won't have anyone to find jobs for me."

"All I want is to get out of the country." Ahmed sighed.

"But you've only just got back."

"I know, but who would want to live here once he has seen what it's like outside. If I could get the money I would never come back."

"Anyway Hassan, you won't have any trouble about getting your fellowship. O'Farrell is new. His friends will tell him he won't find a counterpart unless he offers you a fellowship. "

"Everyone knows that the more people he can persuade to accept scholarships the better his headquarters will like him. That's how they get promotion."

"Yes, someone said they are like traders and are paid by the number of fellowships they get rid of."

The gossip continued round and round the same theme until it was eventually time for the party to break up and return home. Home, which represented to each one of them an environment repugnant in some way or another. Home, where they ate and slept till it was time to return to the aimless official drudgery of the morrow. Home, where they dreamed of life in foreign countries for which alone their higher education seemed to have fitted them.

Eyeball to Eyeball

D. THE VERDICT

The Minister sat at his massive desk burdened with blotters, ball point pens stuck spearlike into their holders, telephones and other status equipment. At the door a servant sat, ready and waiting to obey whatever commands were given him. Hassan, his son, sat, his knees respectfully together, on the other side next to Jelib.

"I am glad that O'Farrell has agreed to give my son a fellowship to go to England, Jelib. We must now keep him happy until he leaves at the end of the year."

"I will do my best, father."

"It will not be easy. He appears to me to be one of these idealists. They are the most difficult to handle as they expect us to follow their advice. They are not content merely to go on drawing their substantial salaries. They must always be pestering us to take action."

He paused and ruminated awhile at the bookcase with its cracked glass. No one had ever read the rows of technical works presented by some wellwishing agency, least of all the Minister himself. They looked handsome at any rate, even though dust lay undisturbed on every ledge and surface.

"Yes" he continued, studying his finger nails "you must convince him that the government intends to introduce this pernicious system of local government. You should ask him to produce his suggestions in detail. Then Jelib will arrange meetings for them to be discussed. There must be plenty of delays between the meetings. Then the plans will be discussed by our Ministerial committees. He must never know that we are not interested in his suggestions."

His cold eyes rested on Jelib who smiled nervously.

"Do not worry, Minister. We know how to handle these matters. If he is awkward, we can always say that the government does not require his advice any longer, and so his contract need not be renewed."

"Quite. If he appears amenable and realistic" he emphasized "then we can recommend his assignment be extended. I think we all understand each other."

The others assured him that they did. By understanding they merely had to bear in mind that the Minister himself was a great land-holder. He wielded, together with his colleagues in the Government who were in like case, absolute power over the people living and working on his estates. This was the only form of local government he understood or was likely to tolerate.

At the same time, the world must be persuaded that the government was taking steps to democratise this feudal system. The appointment of experts to advise it to do so was an earnest of its intentions.

"You must remember" he cautioned "that these foreign agencies are equally happy with this arrangement, for they are able to claim that they are influencing the government to undertake social and administrative reforms. We must at all costs preserve this illusion."

"There is one thing, father. O'Farrell expects me to organize local government when I come back from my course in England."

"You need not worry yourself about that" replied his father. "By that time O'Farrell will be gone and we can give suitable excuses. In any case, I have arranged with my friend the Foreign Minister that when you have finished your training you will be appointed to one of our Embassies abroad. We will explain that this was unavoidable if anyone should question our action. Then I think everyone will be satisfied. You will have the kind of idle occupation that I think appeals to you, Hassan. O'Farrell, if he has any sense, which I doubt, will have enjoyed a year's lucrative employment in unusual surroundings. You, Jelib, will have served the country's interests well. As I know, you are not comfortably blessed with this world's goods, you will appreciate the promotion which will, no doubt, result from your efforts."

"As to this matter of local government," he continued, "We will keep the interest of our overseas friends alive by inviting another Adviser to guide our next steps. It will probably be a question of starting again from the beginning, I am afraid."

As they left the great man's presence, Jelib could not help ruminating that serving one's country was indeed basically a matter of enlightened self-interest.

CHAPTER 9

Community Development

BY TOM

I was still very much in the dark about what the programmes of Community Development in the villages actually consisted. The Head of the Mission had certainly explained the pattern when I first arrived and it was obviously based on the Indian Model with the training of the village level workers to become multipurpose instructors based on village halls. This was a system which had been tried in Kenya after the last war but abandoned with the introduction of rural campaigns of self help based on the traditional practice of group programmes, too arduous to be undertaken by individual farmers, or to be more precise, their wives on their own.

There had been little opportunity to find out in the field when I first arrived as winter was approaching and the villagers were preparing themselves for it by plastering their flat rooves against the spring thaw of snow, and stacking their winter fuel under cover, grinding grain, and so forth.

I was anxious to do a tour of some nearby villages to make a study of all this as soon as spring was on the way and the villagers had got out into the open once the biting frosts had abated. Without this understanding it would be impossible to plan a proper programme and fix priorities for the working season.

I therefore discussed a programme with him and was eager to see how the village workers who had been trained earlier were getting on after their years course. It was agreed to take a party of staff on a study tour during the spring break.

Apparently our leader had impressed the coordinating Committee in Bangkok and it was intending to send a team to evaluate our progress.

In the meanwhile we planned a programme of field work in a neighbouring village on the lines of those group activities which had been so successful in

Eyeball to Eyeball

Kenya. It was to be organised in two parts. The first was to be the reconstruction of a clapper bridge over the Logar River. This was the kind of work they were well accustomed to but which had to be constantly repeated as the spring floods regularly washed them away. Perhaps with the use of cement we could produce a more durable structure.

The second project was more difficult and consisted of an aqueduct. For years the spring floods had carried away the existing channel where one irrigation channel crossed another. As a result it was impossible to cultivate a large area of otherwise fertile land.

We had fortunately two Russians in our team, both of them architects by profession but one officially designated the interpreter of the other - so we had two experts for the price of one. They very kindly agreed to draw up plans for the engineer and we managed to get cement and reinforcing rods released for the job, all labour being provided by the villagers.

On the day appointed for the start of the work, we all went down to the site where the materials and concrete mixers had been collected.

A large number of villagers had already assembled and in the distance was the sound of drumming as the village elders approached.

It was all most exciting as without prompting the villagers had adopted one of the techniques which had made the Kenya Community development schemes so successful - song and dance. Perhaps this traditional way of working is much more widely practised than we had realised.

Excitement was mounting. The villagers separated into groups under the few artizans which were available, and the dust began to rise and billow as the long handled shovels dug into the sandy soil. Water carriers with goat skin bags began to circulate like Gunga Din to the sweating labourers.

Work went on all that week not only on the aqueduct but the distributing system of connecting canals to individual fields until it was finally completed and hardened and ready to be connected to the Logar River. Then the celebrations started, all strictly teetotal as befitted a Muslim community.

The evaluation tour was less encouraging. We visited a number of villages to inspect progress. Not without difficulty we obtained access to the social hall so similar in layout to any village hall in an english country village and so utterly alien to the Afghan Culture. Having gained entrance we made enquiries about

Community Development

the libraries which had been set up only to find them firmly locked and for the same reason that those at the training center were secured - to forestall theft by denying access to their contents.

It was the same story with the agricultural implements, the tools and the seeds, the fertilizer; bureaucracy run riot with the natural consequence of stagnation.

I felt honour bound to report this depressing waste of time and effort by all concerned. The result was not what I had hoped, a round table conference to alter the direction of policy to enable the schemes to reflect the needs of the communities as in the case of the aqueduct. Instead there was only resentment at what was regarded as destructive criticism.

But an even greater disappointment was the fate of the new training center which had been under construction at Bulzar ever since the time of my arrival. Each day we had seen it rising in the compound. A two storey block of what looked like substantial masonry. However our hopes were doomed to disappointment.

On arriving at the center one day I took a walk past the new building and it struck me that the balcony which ran the whole length of the first floor had begun to sag. In fact it was beginning to look like a series of suspension bridges or perhaps a clothes line. What would happen when a crowd of students began to crowd along it?

I immediately decided to drive back to Kabul and report to our Headquarters. Our two Russian architects kindly agreed to come out straight away and make an inspection.

Their report came in next day. The building would have to be condemned immediately. The amount of cement used in its construction was negligible. The Minister and his experts came to inspect and returned sadly shaking their heads but nothing happened. After a week or two I asked my counterpart what action was being taken. Should we put up warning notices in the building. There was no reply.

Eventually he told me the story. "I see you have not been told about our system of approving contracts for public buildings" he observed and I had to agree this was the case. Apparently contracts are not signed with firms which have the highest record of performance or even offer the best financial terms. Favourable consideration was given to the contractor who offered the highest commission to the officials concerned. This was paid on a sliding scale starting with the

Eyeball to Eyeball

Minister and distributed pro rata in accordance with the importance of the individual concerned. "It even applies to me" he concluded with great honesty.

He was later hounded by his superiors for his indiscretion and I had to work very hard to convince everyone concerned what an excellent man he was and how much he had helped me in my work. Perhaps with hindsight this was not a particularly valuable commendation knowing what I had tried to do to clean out the augean stables.

As for me I was not particularly surprised when my contract was not renewed. But I was grateful to be given another similar one, this time in Turkey and under the auspices of the British Government.

CHAPTER 10

The Selang Tunnel

BY TOM

One of my followup tours for former trainees at the Gulzar community development center was to a pilot scheme near the Selang Pass. I did not know much about this area but had been told that a huge tunnel was being bored through the Hindu Kush mountains and its southern exit was at Selang. The pass was a vital point on the North South Highway and was frequently impassable in winter.

At all times of the year however the road was jammed by trucks zigzagging up the mountain side in low gear. The only other route to Russia and the wide northern plains of Herat was far to the west where the mountains began to peter out in the plains of Iran.

It was very historic too and led to places with romantic names such as Tashkent, Bukhara and Samarkand. It also linked with the only pass leading into China through the Lakman pedicle in the Pamir mountains along the Silk Way.

This was the route taken by Alexander in his invasion of India and later by Ghengis Khan and Tamerlane on the same mission. But more significantly than any of these campaigns was the thousand year ambition of Russia for a warm water port on the Indian Ocean wherever it might be, an ambition obstructed first by nature and in more recent times by Britain which jealously guarded the continent of India for three hundred years from other European interlopers.

It is clear now that Russia sought to establish an all weather route to what is now Pakistan via Afghanistan. To do so its engineers came to the conclusion that the only solution was to tunnel under the Hindu Kush in the pretence of opening up a trade route to the North.

We were fortunate to be in Afghanistan during the period immediately preceding the Russo Afghan war, a period when the Americans had decided to plug a gap in Russian Expansionism caused by the withdrawal of Britain from

Eyeball to Eyeball

India in 1947. They decided to do so by trying to persuade the Afghan Governments that its best interests lay with them rather than with Russia but sadly bungled the whole affair. We saw it all developing under our noses, but we were not aware of its significance at the time.

The children were out for their first summer holidays in 1961 and we thought they would enjoy the trip to the Hindu Kush, the wonderful emerald lakes at Bandi Amir and the vast statues of Buddha at Bamian. Sights which the tour operators would give their eyes to make available to the world if they were not completely inaccessible as a result of war and confusion. The only travellers who may still be able to catch a glimpse of these wonders are those following the Hippy Trail, the only peaceful successors of the warlike hoardes which preceded them. So the Salang was to the Russians what the Khyber was to the British.

We made a courtesy call on the Governor of the province and asked him for a permit to visit our project in the Selang. He was very helpful and gave us the required authority. We were glad later that we had obtained it.

Off we drove through delightful park-like country, the mountains towering above us until we reached a barrier. I went into the office of the Guard who stamped our pass. As I walked down to the Landrover, I saw a truck charging down the hill in a cloud of dust. It drew up and the driver began to gesticulate pointing at us.

The guard came over to me and said in a rather embarrassed way that we could go no further. "But we have a permit signed by the Governor" I objected. At this the argument started in Russian.

I suppose I should not have got involved but I got angry and said "Who is running this country? I want to ring up the Governors office and ask him to speak to the Russians." This made the Guard very angry but he rang the Governors office nevertheless and came over to me.

"You may drive on" he announced which we proceeded to do without further comment.

I got the impression that though the Russians had enormous influence, the Afghans resented them asserting their power over their own government it was the first indication that I had had of the undercurrent of feeling that existed between the Russians and the Afghans. In many instances they might even be members of the same tribe which often extended beyond the international

The Selang Tunnel

boundaries. This gave the Russians an advantage over other foreigners but it was not enough where national pride was at stake.

Of course we were careful not to approach the scene of operations of the tunnelling engineers that would only stir up trouble once more when we would find ourselves in the wrong. It was interesting that a few months later a terrible explosion was reported to have occurred in the tunnel which was many miles long and nearing completion. It was rumoured that a trial run of lorries had taken place and hundreds of men had been killed. Whether it was sabotage or an accident we never knew and were not interested. It was sometimes wiser not to dig too deep. The tunnel project had to be abandoned temporarily.

It was not difficult to appreciate the strategic possibilities of such a calamity.

CHAPTER 11

The Great Grape Airlift

BY TOM

The relationship between the various countries which were providing Aid to Afghanistan was obviously of some concern to the United Nations, although the scale of its operations was much smaller than either the Americans or the Russians. After discussions at top level it was decided to divide the programmes geographically with the dividing line roughly east and west through Kabul. The Russians would be responsible for projects north of this line and the Americans south of it.

The Americans thus became responsible for many more projects than the Russians such as the Helmund Valley Irrigation Scheme and the road from Kabul to the Khyber Pass, and the Russians remained responsible for the road from the capital to the Russian border which was vital to them for obvious reasons. When the war broke out, it was clear that the SALANG Tunnel had been a strategic operation and a failure at that. Privately it was comforting to see how many of the more grandiose schemes proved failures for the most elementary reasons.

There was, for instance, a road which had been built by the Russians to connect the King's summer palace at Paghman with the capital sixteen miles away. Within a year or two it began to break up and the Afghan authorities asked the Russians to repair it. This they refused to do and said it was an accepted principle that capital works were the financial responsibility of the donors but their maintenance rested with the host country, which was probably true but it assumed that the works had been carried out properly in the first place.

The Afghan Government then became crafty, and asked the Americans if they would undertake the repair. This they accepted but instead of actually doing so, they built a brand new road alongside to a high specification. They re-erected posters where it started with the usual pictures of American/Afghan hands grasped in symbolic accord. The lesson could hardly be missed and it represented round one to the stars and stripes. The Russians had been outsmarted.

Eyeball to Eyeball

However, round two, which occurred soon after, was a much more bitter contest.

I have mentioned that just before my arrival in Kabul, the Afghan Government had decided to break off diplomatic relations with Pakistan and in fact claimed that the whole of that country was intrinsically Afghan in origin. This was probably true as it had been annexed by the British when they declared it part of the Indian Empire three hundred years before.

The Pakistanis had to decide whether to declare war on Afghanistan or to do the next best thing and break off diplomatic relations and leave it to the Afghans to declare war if they felt like it. They decided this was not worth while. It seems likely that the Russians had advised the Afghans that all they had to do was to sit tight and in due course the Americans, whose lines of communication naturally ran to Kabul through the Khyber Pass, would be unable to continue with their development programme and would have to pull out.

But at this stage another factor entered into the dispute. Autumn was approaching when the vast grape harvest was plucked. The Afghans, being Muslim, did not follow the usual practice of turning it into wine but instead dried it and converted it to raisins. They exported it down the wonderful highway the Americans had built for them from Kabul to the Khyber Pass where it was sold in Pakistan. But what was to happen now that the road had been closed? It was no longer possible to use camels, the trade had become far too big for such an old fashioned form of transport. So what would happen? The Russians were approached and the whole problem waived aside as of no moment. "We will buy the whole harvest", they said reassuringly.

"But how?", asked the Afghans.

"By sending in Illuysin transporter aircraft". The Afghans were much relieved.

But we rather thought from our stand on the touchline that there were others apart from the growers who were becoming disillusioned with the closing of the frontier. While it was closed the Americans had been unable to continue their programme of building schools, roads, or dams, so naturally the contractors found themselves without a job. But of even greater importance, the rewards which no doubt used to bring joy to the various officials connected with the projects came to an end. It was like watching a game of American football without knowing the rules and guessing who was winning by the volume of the cheers.

The Great Grape Airlift

Eventually the day came for the delivery of the raisins to the airport. The approach roads were jammed with lorries which in turn were grossly overloaded with the fruit. The sky was vibrant with the roar of the aircraft landing and taking off continuously day and night. It was a most impressive operation. After a few weeks it was over. It had caused a great impression among the growers and the Russian stock stood very high. But to their disappointment, disillusion eventually dispelled their euphoria; The Russians sent in their account - which was prodigious.

"But it never cost half as much to take the raisins by road", the farmers complained. The Prime Minister and the King were besieged by the farmers whose profits were so much less than normal, by the public who were deprived of the fruits of the American Aid programme, and lastly by the officials who had to forego their rake-offs.

"This stupid embargo must stop", they cried and very soon afterwards the lorries began to grind their way once more up the miracle of American engineering, the Devil's Gully, on the road from Peshawar to Kabul and the Aid programme gathered momentum once more. Did this experiment in Strategic Diplomacy lead to the invasion of Afghanistan a few years later? For us onlookers, it was an experience similar to the Berlin Airlift, but in that case the aircraft won.

Diplomatic relations were restored to the relief of all concerned, except perhaps that of the Russians. We were bitterly disappointed not to have been flies on the wall when the negotiations were being undertaken and had to rely on supposition.

It was of course very trying for us personally. The breaking of diplomatic relations occurred when our luggage and car were actually on the water en route for Karachi. This meant that we had to buy a duplicate stock of furniture bedding etc etc, an expensive if fascinating ploy. It was amazing what you could find if you first found the appropriate suk. For blankets one had to go to the bedding suk, and we found many wonderful locally made ones with red and green stripes a centimeter thick. As Patricia has described we had our "easy" furniture made in the one which sold rope strung couches and chairs.

Mercifully after about six months of this economic blockade the government allowed a chink to appear. The owners of stranded cars were tipped the wink to go off flat out for Karachi which lay 1500 miles to the south before someone decided to shut the frontier once more.

Eyeball to Eyeball

We flew to Karachi via Delhi and then found our way by decrepit taxi to the docks with some trepidation. What would our cars be like after 6 months on the quayside in blistering heat. To our astonishment they were in firstclass condition and virtually ready for the road. A local garage filled them up with fuel and oil, put some air in the somewhat deflated tyres, cleaned the windscreen and we were ready for the "off".

Fortunately, I had a certain amount of experience of long distance travel over earth roads in tropical heat. Some years before, after a few months leave in South Africa, Patricia and I decided to buy a second hand Ford V8 and drive the six thousand miles back to Kenya over even worse roads than the Asiatic ones. We got the best tip from a sales representative in Ladysmith who advised us to do what the experts had strongly advised us against - to bleed the tyres and reduce the pressure which built up with each hour from pounding over the corrugations and pot holes. In consequence we never had a single puncture or blow out and only one broken spring. With little traffic, driving had its particular hazards however, particularly in the Punjab, where the road ran along bends between the paddy fields. Here we met a succession of carts drawn by water buffaloes which obviously knew this road backwards as the drivers were invariably fast asleep in what went for the cab. One had to use ones horn a great deal, more to wake up the drivers than to persuade them to get across to the proper side of the road.

It was even more difficult at night because the only warning we got of the presence of a cart was its lantern swinging beneath. One had to drive at night however because of our race against time. It might make all the difference between being shut out at the Khyber when and if we ever reached it.

Driving in the day time was much more attractive particularly with the sight of the farmers trotting along to the next town. With the husband seated on the front hump of their vast Bactrian camels and his wife on the back one as if on a pillion. He was a magnificent sight in his turban and neatly cut beard and she modest and demure, her sari blowing about in the breeze.

We gave up any idea of staying together and said goodbye at the outskirts of Karachi and hoped to meet again in Kabul in a weeks time. It was a long slog in great heat.

As I drove into the outskirts of Peshawar I noticed a surprising sight. What was very clearly an army officer trotting along the verge in his white breeches, black boots and helmet, returning from a game of polo. He would not have looked out of place at Hurlingham. And then as we approached the centre of the town one began to see the statues of Generals at the cross-roads and could not help wondering if a carriage might not appear at any moment taking some ladies to visit their friends, parasols poised over their heads.

Later on we would be visiting Peshawar quite frequently in search of warmth when the weather became bitter in winter time. At first we stayed in a hotel but then a friend asked why we did not use the Club.

"Well I doubt if we could reciprocate with the Kabul International Club" I objected.

"Why not, you're British aren't you?" It seemed a bit of a non-sequitor.

Nevertheless I thought there was no harm in calling on the Secretary. He could not have been more friendly and assured me that we would be most welcome. I shall always remember our first visit. We were shown to a table for dinner placed on an immaculate lawn under a starry sky, the only sound being a low murmuring from the servants waiting to attend to us and the pulsating whirring of a huge electric fan placed by each table to circulate the listless air.

The meal was naturally delicious and when it was over the Head Steward came to ask if we had enjoyed it. It was a somewhat superfluous question.

"Would you care for a game of billiards" he enquired "to end the evening."

"Well thank you, but my wife does not play" I replied with a smile.

"But the marker would be very happy to give you a game" he urged and I could not refuse, although I knew that I should be slaughtered, which is exactly what happened. On our way back we paused at that 'Holy of Holies' the horseshoe bar, still immaculately polished but deserted. The days when Officers in mess jackets crowded round it had gone forever.

Nevertheless the goodwill remained. British Generals continued to bestride their horses at the cross-roads. Three hundred years of close association is not wiped out so easily as that. The people of the Indies have grown accustomed to foreign invasion and strangely enough do not appear to resent exploitation or the depredations of nature. It is even possible that they put greater faith in the powers of God than in that of politicians.

CHAPTER 12

Memories of Afghanistan

BY MICHAEL

Road to Jellalbad

My memories of Afghanistan started with the trip which Jos, Marcus and I made by a KLM Lockheed Electra from Amsterdam to Teheran at the beginning of the summer holidays of 1962. I was sixteen and at Pangbourne, Marcus was thirteen and must have just started at Haileybury, and Jos was nineteen, and working in London. We stayed at the Semiramis hotel in downtown Teheran, and I was amazed by the sheer luxury of accommodation. The next day we went by an Afghan Airways DC4 to Kabul, flying over miles and miles of brown desert, a voyage apparently to the middle of nowhere. Kabul airport was a modest and decrepit affair made up of a control tower and some scruffy, unpainted buildings, with a large number of Afghans milling around. We were met there by Ma and Pa, whom we hadn't seen for

Eyeball to Eyeball

about six months. I remember that Pa had lost a lot of weight, due it seems to unsanitary conditions in the UN hostel.

We drove to our new house, a mud-walled bungalow totally enclosed from the street. Ma and Pa had only recently moved into it, but they had fitted it out well with nice kilim cushions and low chairs. It had a small verandah where we had our meals, looking out over a square of grass, surrounded by vines growing on a framework to provide shade. Abdul was the houseboy and cook, and had learned how to make a few dishes from his former French employers, including "compot" or stewed fruit. I remember our breakfasts on the balcony, eating cereal with diluted powdered milk.

Us kids of course did not know anyone in Kabul, and so the Kabul International Club was a vital place for meeting people, and to enjoy the pool and the tennis courts. We swam and played a lot. "Bachas" or "boys" were always on hand to help out as ball boys. Two people I remember meeting there were a French boy of my age who was lucky enough to have a Honda 50 motor bike, and an American with the splendid name of Dexter Miracle. Kabul had some wonderful markets and food stalls, and plenty of places where one could buy ethnic arts and crafts. I remember getting a multi-coloured embroidered hat, a striped Afghan coat to serve as a dressing gown, an embroidered sheepskin waistcoat, whose smell could never be got rid of, and no doubt some other souvenirs. I also remember watching a massive military parade, with waves of vehicles, weapons and troops going past us. It could have been a parade in Red Square, Moscow.

Afghanistan in the 1960s was an interesting place. Geographically, it was located between the USSR in the north and Pakistan and Iran to its west, south and east. It was fiercely proud of its independence and had never been colonized. The contrast between the starched military and police uniforms of its Pakistani neighbours, and its own ones showed which side the British had made an impact. Politically, Afghanistan was coveted by both the western and eastern blocs. Both the former USSR and the USA poured in vast amounts of aid, with sometimes questionable impact. It was mused that the Russians came in first and built a road, which then had to be improved and enlarged by the Americans when it started to deteriorate. Then both sides were accused of building massive white elephants, the extreme one being the international airport in Kandahar, which was hardly justified by the current or projected air traffic.

Pa was working as a UN expert, trying to train community development workers, at a new centre at Gulzar, which was still under construction. I

Memories of Afghanistan

remember him being picked up every morning by a Russian jeep, with his Afghan interpreter, and describing how he sometimes had to organize physical training (PT) exercises at the start of the day to warm the students up, since there was not heating. It was evident that the Afghans were way behind Kenya in terms of understanding and practice of community development principles, and the assignment was not an easy one. The difficult weather conditions in winter also did not help, but life was greatly improved by the strong expatriate presence of aid workers, with whom Ma and Pa made many friends. He was an active member of the KADS, the Kabul Amateur Dramatic Society, and was always full of interesting Afghan stories.

When we were there, we had an opportunity to make a few trips. I still remember a trip we made to Charikar, forty miles north of Kabul, where there was a UN tanning expert. We visited the tannery, which was the object of his advice, and the smell is something which can still be remembered. He and his wife were extremely hospitable, and we were spoilt by some of their rich curries, and sweets which his wife made for us.

We made a trip to Bamyan, the spectacular green valley flanked by two massive Buddhas, over a hundred feet high, carved out of the cliff face, whose faces had been cut out hundreds of years ago by Moslem invaders. We also went to Bandi Amir, a gorgeous blue lake, whose side had been built up over thousands of years as a result of the deposit of limestone (?) contained in the water. The lake was a real oasis, a spot of brilliant blue in a vast area of brown, lacking any signs of vegetation. I believe that I was bold enough to have a swim, and the water was bitterly cold.

The most memorable part of our two months stay in Afghanistan was our family holiday in Kashmir. To get there we drove in our Peugeot 403 from Kabul east to Jalallabad, and then down through the Khyber Pass to Peshawar. I shall never forget the sight of the shields of British regiments which had been carved into the side of the Khyber Pass, or set in cement, vestiges of British presence on the North-West Frontier earlier in the century. Further reminders of this were evident in the military club we stayed at in Peshawar. Formerly a bastion of the British officer class, and now taken over by the Pakistan army, the billiard tables, the squash courts, and the tennis courts were being used by new generations of officers, and the bar propped up officers who almost spoke with the same accent. One poignant reminder of the end of the Raj were the many boards showing the winners of various club competitions, on which entries of names seemed to stop in 1947. It seemed difficult to believe that the Pakistanis did not continue with the same competitions.

Eyeball to Eyeball

From Peshawar, we drove east across northern Pakistan to Lahore, miles and miles of hot and humid plains, with the only relief being available when the car was driving along with all the windows open. In Lahore, we drove through a thriving city, with magnificent old buildings dating from the Raj, and the famous "Kim's gun" still in position. We then crossed the border into India and spent the night at a guest house in Amritsar, where we left the car before flying north to Srinagar, in Kashmir.

When in Amritsar, we visited the Golden Temple, the holy shrine of Sikhs. I still remember the exquisite beauty of the Temple, and its golden domes, situated in the middle of a lake and only accessible via a causeway. Nearby, was a massive food hall, where anybody in need could receive a meal for free, a remarkable symbol of Sikh generosity to needy brethren. I remember learning about the five characteristics of a Sikh: that they would never cut their hair, that they would wear a silver bracelet at all times, that they have a dagger available on their person, and a couple of other rituals of belief.

The next day we flew up by Indian Airlines DC3 to Srinagar, where we were due to have a week's holiday on a houseboat on the Dal Lake. Our boat was called "Pigeon". It was one of dozens lined up on the edge of the lake which used to be rented to the British seeking respite in Kashmir from the summer heat of the plains. But we were among the very few tourists in Srinagar at that time, a depressing sign of a declining industry. But this did not deter us from enjoying the holiday. The houseboat was beautifully fitted out with all mod cons, and furniture, and was very comfortable. There was also a full-time cook. The only snag was that we all went down with a fierce outbreak of diarrhea, due we felt to unsanitary conditions in the kitchen.

While there, we used to go on boat rides into the Dal lake, teeming with huge lotus flowers and lilies. On one occasion, we hired horses and went for a long trek up into the mountains to a former hill station. Built by and for the Raj, this station was still intact, except that it was empty. The golf course was deserted and the hotels were vacant, a vivid reminder of a past way of life.

We also went into Srinagar for shopping, and Ma and Pa bought a beautiful carpet, as well as some carved wooden items, and painted boxes, which we still have.

After the holiday, we return to Amritsar, and made our way back to Kabul, the same way as we had come, an unforgettable two weeks away for all of us.

Memories of Afghanistan

Our single visit to Afghanistan was a special one for all of us. Afghanistan has always had a special place in our hearts as a very exotic place in which to live, and one which we were privileged to be able to visit. It was a unique country, visually stunning, culturally very different from any we had been in, and with remarkable people who were unlike any we had known before.

Michael Askwith

23 November 1997

Bandi Amir Salt Lake

PART 2

TURKEY

Tours made and places referred to in the text.

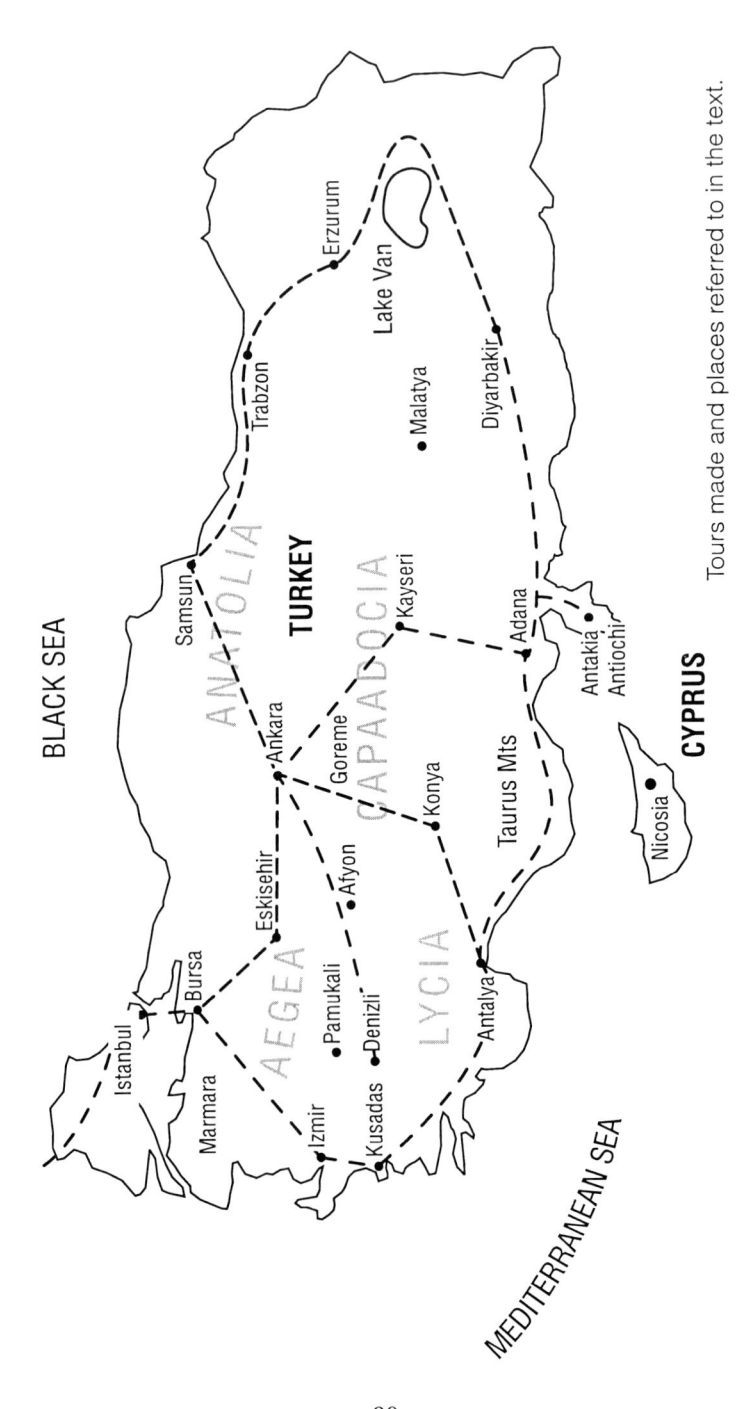

PART 2

Turkey

Ankara Castle

INTRODUCTION

BY TOM

I can't say that our departure from Kabul was a particularly cheerful occasion, but I suppose it was much on a par with our arrival. Our colleagues came down to the airport to see us off. One could not help wondering what would become of our decrepit training centre at Gulzar and what would happen to the students - it would be more disappointing for them than anyone else. They had been so enthusiastic during our short period when

Eyeball to Eyeball

they had seen the results of the project on the paddy fields, and so optimistic that it might be repeated in their own home areas in due course.

As for ourselves, we had to think what we could do to meet the children's school fees and so eke out our pension. I had ideas of starting a sailing school and we bought a house in Restronquet Creek where we thought we could base it. As had so often happened before, we received still one more invitation to work abroad and this was virtually the last. The Turkish government wanted their community development programme evaluated. To do this they wanted an assessment made of the effectiveness of the various projects they had started. This seemed to be an interesting assignment and we decided to accept it. On this occasion my employer would be the British government however, although I would be reporting to the Turkish government and would be working in the Prime Minister's office in Ankara.

The section to which I was posted went by the imposing title of **Toplum Kalkum Mase**. This consisted of representatives of a number of Ministries; Education, Health and Agriculture and so on. The head and co-ordinator of this body was a charming lady whose mother had the distinction of being the first lady graduate at the University of Istanbul and was herself similarly qualified.

I owe her a great debt for her advice and guidance in many directions on my first arrival. But I was mystified at first that the government had decided to appoint a woman as the leader of the group. It seemed a surprising choice for an Islamic government in a male oriented and indeed a military based society to do. But she was very frank in her explanation and pointed out that if any one of the other members of the group had been chosen, jealousies and resentments might have been encouraged and so the wise move was taken to select a co-ordinator rather than a leader and in my view a better choice could not have been made. Lela had a remarkable ability of preserving good will among us.

I received little guidance on how to tackle the task of evaluating the programme and so during the first two years of my assignment I decided to walk like Agag - very delicately, after all Turkey was a very proud nation and not unlike my own in this respect. What is more, until comparatively recently it had been the ruler of a large empire stretching as far as Persia in the east and the borders of Egypt in the south, Algeria and Tripoli in the west and Austria/Hungary in the north west. Possibly the most sensitive portion of their junctures was that with Russia on the Black Sea in the north.

Obviously there was a multiplicity of corns ready to be trodden on, not least perhaps that I was an Englishman whose fatherland had been at war with Turkey

Turkey

not long before and what is more on the winning side. Perhaps this was an advantage however, in some ways.

As an example, I remember we were once having a picnic in the beautiful park-like country which overlooks the Sea of Marmara. It was spring and somewhat chilly and the shepherd, herding his large flock of Angora (Ankara) sheep in the pastures below, was still wearing his rectangular sheepskin cloak. His large dogs roved constantly on guard on the fringes of his flock. Their purpose was to guard the flock and, as a protection, they had been fitted with spiked collars which, if bitten by a wolf, would probably have done it a great deal of harm. This was the lambing season, so they had to be very careful. Later on we acquired one of these collars which we saw on sale in a village market. One had no idea what it was at the time, but were told it was designed to protect the necks of the sheep dogs. Each link consisted of a murderous spike which lay embedded and hidden in the thick mane of the dog. It reminded me of the classical portrayals of Cerberus and no doubt this design had been retained, unchanged, since Diana hunted in these very pastures, a couple of millennia ago.

Meanwhile, we continued to munch our ham sandwiches and survey the drowsy scene. The flock came closer and closer until at last the shepherd was near enough to greet us.

"Merhaba! Masle sin is".

"How are you?"

I aired my newly and inadequately acquired Turkish and started the inevitable probing into our respective origins.

Were we Germans?, who comprised the bulk of foreign tourists.

No English.

A look of surprise and even friendliness appeared on his face.

"You do not seem to see many Englishmen perhaps" I suggested.

"No, not for many years - but I used to do", he replied. "I fought them", and he roared with laughter.

Eyeball to Eyeball

"They used to give me cigarettes", he continued. This opened up a host of possible memories. Down there where the sun was glinting on the water lay the Dardanelles. Could our friend have fought there? It was only fifty years ago after all. My newly acquired Turkish was unfortunately not up to it. But we could ask him to join our meal which he did with avidity, ham or no ham. One way or another we made friends and shared memories and the meeting epitomises, for me, the five delightful and rewarding years we spent in Turkey.

CHAPTER 13

The Sick Man of Europe

BY TOM

This was the title given to Turkey when I was still at school. The country was suffering from a general malaise, but then so was the whole of Europe in the aftermath of the First Great War. The Allies had promised the Arabs their independence from the Ottoman Empire in return for their support in the desert war. So, in due course, Turkey was left with a depleted and impoverished population. Trade to the Far East had been declining steadily for many years as the sea routes had taken the place of the camel caravans. She had one asset however, she was allied to the host of people who inhabited the area extending from China to the Black Sea, many of whom were ready to migrate westwards if given the opportunity.

In this period, just before the Second World War, the people of China were engaged in a long, drawn-out Civil War between those who supported the new doctrine of communism which had spread from Russia, and the more conservative followers of Mao Tse Tung.

The inhabitants of a certain village in Sinkiang Province situated on the western borders of China, found themselves with no alternative but to escape across the Himalayas and take refuge in Kashmir which was at that time under British rule. It was a strange coincidence that they found themselves marooned not far from the crossing of the ways at the Wakhan Pass where the Marco Polo or Silk Trail cleaves the pedicle through the Pamir mountains and where so many invading forces have either found a route to India from Mongolia as in the case of Ghengis Khan or from Turkey in the case of Alexander the Great. It is in fact the Piccadilly Circus of Central Asia and almost as dangerous.

A complication arose with the end of the Raj and the authorities were faced with the problem with what to do with the refugees until an official remembered seeing an announcement about an offer of asylum which the Turkish government had announced to deal with the situation of exactly this nature.

Eyeball to Eyeball

Accordingly, in due course, the villagers found themselves boarding alarming looking vehicles with vast wings attached to their sides. But they faced the situation with perfect equanimity and in fact with surprising cheerfulness.

It reminded me of a situation which occurred when the Jewish government was providing facilities for their countrymen who had been long domiciled in the Arabian Peninsular to return to their fatherland. As in the case of the refugees from Sinkiang they showed no apprehension at the prospect of taking to the air. However, a member of the aircraft crew became seriously alarmed when he noticed the smell of burning emanating from the cargo bay where the Jews were accommodated. He opened the door and was met by a cloud of smoke. In the middle of it he made out a group of figures crouched on the floor of the plane around what appeared to be a cooking stove. He sounded the alarm and every available fire extinguisher was brought into play.

His language can be imagined when he demanded an explanation for their recklessness, but there was no common means of communication and his fulminations fell on deaf ears.

Eventually it transpired that the reason why the émigrés were treating the aircraft like home was that indeed they regarded it as such. According to their traditions, they were convinced that one day they would be transported to the promised land on the wings of an eagle - this was obviously it.

But to return to our account of our effort to revise the rural economy in Turkey, the experiences of our refugees from China will provide a very good object lesson.

I have mentioned that our team of specialists had worked out a plan to visit all the provinces in turn and hold what in the parlance of the time were referred to as seminars. These took place in the local school or college and we slept in one of the dormitories if it was holiday time. All the technical staff attended and were lectured on what could have been achieved by self-help in the various fields and then discussed how these lessons would be applied.

It reminded me of my last task before leaving Kenya which was to visit Malawi or Nyasaland as it was referred to at that time, at the request of the government and to describe our experiences in Kenya in this particular direction. As in the case of Turkey, where we operated under the authority of the head of the province, the Governor or Wali, I was fortunate in having the support of my old rowing pal, Robin, later to be Sir Robert Foster. All inter-departmental obstacles were therefore swept away and we operated on a united front. We had one philosophy, to develop the spirit of self-help which is to be found amongst so many communities throughout the world if it is only given the right encouragement.

Let us take our Chinese refugees as an example again therefore. When they first arrived in Istanbul they were put into a camp to await the completion of the village where they would be living in due course. While they were there the young people were given courses in handicrafts which were mainly in connection with the tourist trade. They were taught to make leather goods and the girls household decorative articles of all kinds.

In due course the village was ready for occupation and plans for the move to their desolate new home in the wastes of Anatoliya were worked out. Each household was to be given a plough and other agricultural tools and a plot of land to cultivate and would then have to fend for themselves.

The government was disappointed that these proposals were not welcomed with delight, but the villagers were disappointed they were apparently not to be encouraged to continue with their newly learned skills. The young men came up with the proposal. Instead of planning their lives in the traditional lines of a peasant community, they proposed that the money given to provide themselves with ploughs and oxen should be pulled and used instead for the purchase of a tractor or two and mechanical implements. Five families would then grow the food required for the whole village.

In addition some of the initial grant would be used to develop a cottage industry for the manufacturing and sale of handicrafts.

The technical officers were a bit nonplussed by these unorthodox proposals. The Turkish government thrives on red tape of which thousands of yards must have been produced every year. But to its credit it agreed to make an exception in this case. What is more, they agreed to give a loan for the construction of a water pump and save women many hours of work fetching and carrying to their houses and giving them more time to weave carpets and make handicrafts.

The loan was to be refunded strictly within five years. It must be emphasised that the government officials were highly suspicious of the scheme. It smacked too much of communism and they anticipated its early decline. But when our teams visited the village with the Vali and all his senior officials with him, we had a very pleasant surprise.

Eyeball to Eyeball

The whole community was seated in a wide semi-circle. In the centre were the elders in their Chinese cloaks and round embroidered caps. They still retained their long beards whereas the middle aged were now clean shaven.

The Vali was given a welcoming address and was thanked for the help he had given them. The last instalment of the five year loan was handed over but the chairman of the village committee asked if a second loan could be given on the same terms. This time however, they wished to install a power plant to generate electricity.

The Governor, as usual a military man, almost exploded. What did a simple village in the depths of the plain want with electricity and luxuries like that? The chairman politely pointed out that lighting in their homes would enable them to work longer and increase their output of articles for sale. They would of course repay the loan as promptly as on the first occasion.

The Governor's objection melted away and in due course modernity arrived which indeed was an axiom first introduced by Ataturk himself when he invented a new Turkish word, "moderne", to be added to the national dictionary.

The number of similar schemes multiplied and helped to meet the ever growing demands of the rapidly expanding tourist industry. Telephone lines for instance began to snake their way across the plains. The poles were cut and carried by the villagers themselves, while the official technicians undertook the wiring and installation. Fuel for the road building machinery was provided in the same way in partnership with the government.

But a tendency began to develop for villagers to move into the towns as elsewhere in the world. In this way social and economic services could be provided more cheaply and efficiently.

Now the country people have for centuries had practiced self-help. When a young man married, his neighbours used to cultivate a coppice of popular trees which were to provide the son with timber in due course to build himself, a new house.

Adapting themselves to changing needs, this practise was used to provide housing in the towns for the villagers wishing to become urbanised. But the authorities became apprehensive to the tendency of villagers building shanty towns in the outskirts of cities. Legislation was introduced to make it an offence to build shacks and took steps to demolish them when they sprang up.

But the country people were a match for the authorities. The tradition of mutual corporation being strong, families would band together and collect the materials needed to build a house and assemble it on the site they had acquired, quite legally, as long as the new house was not left half completed overnight. Then, on an appointed day, they all collected at dawn and built the home in frantic speed until it was completed in triumph as the sun sank below the horizon.

The operation acquired a name "Gechikondo" in European script or self-help housing. Thus an indigenous movement not entirely approved of by the authorities, but nevertheless fulfilling a felt need, which they were reluctant to discourage, helped to pave the way to a more sophisticated and self-sufficient way of life which was in accordance with the principles of community development. I tried to analyse this movement in terms of the experience of more economically advanced nations, based on the principles of self-government, which is the foundation upon which true democracy is based. This is included in an appendix for those who are interested in the process.

CHAPTER 14

Finding a Way

BY TOM

Our group had two objectives. The first was to suggest to the country people and their leaders, how they might rebuild their country and make it prosperous after the bitterness of two World Wars. History teaches us that neighbouring states, tend to rend and devour the defeated with the utmost ruthlessness. Turkey had the same bitter experience as Germany in this respect. What is more, minority groups who had cohabited the country for centuries like the Greeks and Armenians took advantage of the dissolution of the Turkish Empire to satisfy their nationalist ambitions.

Our second task was therefore to evaluate what had been achieved in the past, in relation to the experience of other nations.

Turkey is a vast country stretching a thousand miles from the border of Iran in the east to Serbia in the west and bounded by the Black Sea in the north and the Mediterranean in the south. In between stretches the plateau of the Anatollean Plain over which waves of conquerors from the east had surged since the dawn of time.

In the period following the First World War, the Greeks tried to assert their control of the rich agricultural plain between the Mediterranean and the Taurus mountains, while Armenians and Kurds laid claim to the mountainous parts along the Russian border.

Kemal Attaturk was in command of the Turkish army in its counter-attack and restored the sense of self-respect and pride of the entire nation. This continues to this day and one sees evidence of it in a number of remarkable ways.

Our development group used to make a point of visiting areas which had made particular progress. One of these happened, to be situated in the area of the Sea of Marmara. The head of the local Gendarmerie happened to have taken a considerable interest in local government and had also constructed a kind of

Eyeball to Eyeball

memorial or shrine to commemorate Kemal Attaturk in the lobby of his headquarters many years after the General's death; there were the usual photographs and mementoes and a bust of the great man. But this was remarkable in one respect - the date of his birth was inscribed below but with no date of death. I commented on this, wondering whether it had been erected before his death. No, I was corrected, the reason was apparently that the local people were still not convinced that he had actually died, and wished to reassure themselves that his name would continue to be remembered in perpetuity. In fact this still seems to be so today as we have noticed on return visits to the country which we have made from time to time. His portrait appears everywhere and seems to operate like a talisman in giving encouragement in difficult times. Whether this actually has the desired effect is questionable, as it seems rather to foster a sense of animosity which is still noticeable, particularly between the Turks and the Greeks and Kurds.

On the other hand contrary emotions seemed to be aroused among different sections of the population. For instance Kemal Attaturk was an ardent European emotionally but by no means a strict Muslim. He was a heavy drinker, for instance, and died of cirrhosis of the liver. He was born in Salonika and thus imbued with pro-European sentiments. At the same time he felt that Islam had a retarding influence on the development of the country. There is a story that in order to counteract the conservative influence of the priests he barred the fez, substituting the peaked cap in its place. He thought that in this way the country people would no longer be able to touch the ground with their foreheads in the attitude of prayer, as ordained by the Prophet. The peasants however, simply turned their caps round, back to front, with the peak at the back and so defeated the object of the exercise.

But though a traditionalist he was no conservative. He was indeed a passionate nationalist and did everything he could to rebuild the population depleted by the various wars to expel the Greeks. The priests would have liked to see town clocks abolished in fact, so that they would be left with the final decision regarding the correct time of the day or night. But the radio now has the last word in deciding this issue.

But to return to our campaign of enlightenment, we operated through the normal machinery of government and aimed to hold seminars in each of the Provinces in turn to which all the technical officers would be invited.

Now Turkey was governed in a somewhat autocratic manner. Each Province was governed by a Wali who was invariably a retired general, rather on the lines of a Lord Lieutenant in England. Though in our time in Turkey the Prime

Finding a Way

Minister was usually a civilian, this was not always the case. The President in our time was General Ismet Inonu, Kemal Attaturk's close companion and ally. The army was therefore always lurking in the wings and ready to step in and take control should the government show itself to be too left-wing.

Although the government showed itself to be fairly liberal in outlook it was at the same time suspicious of communist influences making themselves felt from the other side of the Black Sea. On the other hand the social policies from across the water inevitably made themselves felt. This after all has been the tendency of the twentieth century, while democracy was the accepted pattern of government, authoritarianism was equally respected. The attitude of the army inevitably set the pattern of the civil service. It was not surprising therefore, that the influence of Germany was considerable although this was severely dented by its defeat in the First World War and this probably led Turkey to remain unaligned in the second.

It seemed to be a feature of the interwar period that whenever the government was embarrassed by internal unrest, it's propaganda machines were switched to discredit it's traditional enemies, the Greeks and the Armenians. This was not surprising in the case of the latter for in an opportunist manner they decided to extend the boundaries of the mother country at a time when Turkey was reeling from the effects of defeat after the First World War.

Much play was given to the Armenian atrocities which were a feature of the punitive action of the Turks in the Van province at this time, but less to the tragic results of the conflict.

The Armenians had been remarkable agriculturists and had constructed a widespread system of irrigation in the mountains surrounding Lake Van. With the wholesale expulsion of the inhabitants to their homeland, their place was taken by Kurds who later constituted a similar threat to that of the Armenians. They however, were pastoralists and allowed the marvellous irrigation system of their predecessors to go to wrack and ruin as I saw with my own eyes.

The case of the Greeks was somewhat different. The occasion was the Cypriot war of independence. This provided the Greeks with an opportunity to make a claim for the island as part of its national heritage.

We happened to be staying in the attractive town of Samsun at the time. Our hotel overlooked the square and so we were ideally situated to watch the extraordinary events which took place there one sunny morning. There was a great deal of banging going on; trucks trundled over the cobbies with loads of

Eyeball to Eyeball

Samsun

timber and other materials. I asked the staff what was happening, but got only evasive and somewhat embarrassed replies. First of all a dais seemed to be under construction, then flag staffs began to go up; Ministry of Information vans appeared and began erecting stands for their cameras; Little men with pots of paint began to draw lines on the cobbles; Chairs and benches appeared, presumably for the dignitaries. It must be some kind of political meeting, always a popular activity in Turkey at weekends. Then long crocodiles of school children emerged from narrow streets and were drawn up along the white lines; Turkish flags were distributed by busy teachers; Officials fussed around to decide where to place the chairs and tables. It was fascinating to guess what was the plan behind all these preparations. The local populace, such as they were, seemed as mystified as we were, but it provided entertainment for the coffee drinkers in the lokantas along the sides of the square.

At last the "crowds" began to appear and arranged themselves behind the children. It was not unlike a film set and not in the least spontaneous but then it began to dawn on us, it must be some kind of demonstration. Carpenters had begun to erect posters behind the dias and placards distributed among the "crowd". The onlookers were still pretty sparse and the coffee drinkers remained seated at their little tables rather as if they had seen it all before but were interested to check how this performance might compare with the last one.

Finding a Way

Finally, rather important looking cars began to roll up. Out of them emerged military gentlemen dusting down their uniforms; others in suits were obviously city councillors, the rest were policemen in their jeeps.

They all marched to the dais and found their official seats, the loud speakers began to crackle in their familiar way, snatches of music broke the silence and we were off with the national anthem. It was a masterpiece of stage-management. No doubt when the ceremony was later broadcast the viewers must have imagined they were witnessing a vast concourse of loyal Turkish citizens asserting their outrage at Greek effrontery in claiming the island of Cyprus as their own territory. But it was fascinating nevertheless to watch a perfect example of a crowd being actually manipulated before our eyes. With a few props and appropriate scenery the illusion had been created of a vast resentful crowd expressing its democratic rights to the world at large.

Some years later we witnessed an almost identical situation in the Russian sector of Berlin. This was on a somewhat larger scale, but was similar in character to conform with the requirements of the capital. But the pattern might have been derived from any text book on the organisation of "rentacrowd" demonstrations, if such a one exists as I have no doubt that it does, somewhere or other. My brother happened to be stationed in Berlin at this time and we visited him and were amused to hear that the Turks in this instance seemed to have stolen a march on the Russians. While political objectives vary from country to country propaganda to achieve them seems to have much in common.

But to return to our impression of the background of Turkey against which we were working, there is no need to describe it in detail. All the reader requires is a general impression of the historical past.

Turkey has for centuries been regarded as the gateway for Europeans seeking to enter Asia before the sea lanes had been opened up, just as it has been the means of access of traders transporting the scarce products of the East to the capitals of Europe. Alexander the Great crossed the vast Anatollean plain and the deserts of Pursia and found a passage through the Hindu Kush to India which became known as the Silk Road. The Turks and Kindred Tribes from China and Mongolia returned the complement and penetrated Europe as far as the gates of Vienna.

Turkey became the wide corridor between the two continents for those seeking plunder or trade, until eventually supplanted by the navigators who pioneered the sea routes. During our time in Turkey, whether in the course of our task to

Eyeball to Eyeball

assist the development of the country or as tourists, we covered much of this corridor between the Black Sea and the Mediterranean.

It was not the fact that different communities became stabilised that led to the various trails becoming demarcated but simply trade. One of the earliest was what we have come to refer to as the Marco Polo Route or the Silk Route. This was the most important. We made a point of visiting as many of it's caravansaries as possible. They were sited some fourteen miles apart, this distance apparently was as far as the great Bakhtrian camels could manage in a day. The buildings resemble cathedrals and included a forecourt which provided accommodation for the camp followers and those who served them, like the farriers, smiths, tent makers, bakers, butchers and the like. Then there were the permanent guards for protection and the armed escort who conducted the caravan from one Khan to the next and entertainers, cooks, the water carriers and the carers for the sick, a very large community.

Behind the forecourt lay the stabling for the beasts of burden. They were housed in the long building which writers still refer to as the nave and side aisles which were similar to the crossing or lantern in a cathedral. I have often tried to find out the significance of this design. Was it a copy of early Christian architecture or vice versa? The original mosques seemed to have been chiefly circular in shape. Everyone seems agreed that the load carriers were tethered and fed in the side aisles. There must have been heating for them too for winters were bleak on the Anatollean Plateau. There were no windows in the outer walls which were sometimes built of chequered pink stonework, sometimes of cut stone from some earlier Roman building. There was only one gateway, presumably in the interest of security.

The leaders of the caravans would have to pay a fee for their nights lodging so the cost of travelling the 5000 miles, about half of which being spent in crossing China itself, must have been prodigious. In addition there was the provisioning of the camels, not to mention the cost of manhandling the china, silk, opium and other trade goods. The rulers of the various countries through which the caravans passed undoubtedly levied their dues in the time honoured way. A visit to Top Kapi in Istanbul, reveals how much was donated. Shelf after shelf of priceless china is on display there and case after case of jewellery. These were the source of the Sultan's wealth and a measure of the importance of maintaining the Silk Road. Like the ports of call established later by the maritime nations to provision their trading vessels along the sea routes to the Far East, so cities arose along the camel tracks, not least those with romantic names like Bukhara, Tashkent and Samarkand. At the European end apart from Istanbul, other bases became established from which the treasure from the East

Finding a Way

was shipped to Venice and other European ports to evade the highway robbers in the mountains of Greece, who would prey upon the traders as they passed through. I never expected to get an insight into the activities of such individuals and it was well worth the effort to do so.

Like most people who made Turkey their temporary home I acquired a copy of that classic "Mehmet my Hawk" which describes the life of an Asian Robin Hood who spent his life robbing travellers in the interests of the poor. I and some of my Turkish colleagues were motoring in Eastern Turkey on our way to visit the Van area on one occasion, when a development project was being planned.

We were winding our way along a pitted track through the mountains when we were confronted by two magnificent creatures armed to the teeth, slung about with bandoliers and clothed in embroidered waist coats and turbans. We had no option but to stop while the brigands peered into the car.

I had no doubt that at least we would be relieved of any valuables we might be carrying so it was a surprise when after lengthy interrogation about our purpose and origins we were waved ahead with huge grins and much good humour.

"Well, what was all that about?", I enquired.

"It was lucky you were driving the car and not a Turk", they laughed.

Apparently they had agreed between themselves as to whether to rob us or not, but decided it would cause more trouble than it was worth to the local population. The governor had given warning that should any foreigners be troubled by the bandits, he would call out the troops and levy a heavy fine. It was all apparently due to the concern of the government that the country should not get a bad name and so affect it's tourist trade.

Incidentally, the route we were following was one of the oldest in Turkey and was one of the few passes giving access to Iran and the Far East for both motor vehicles and railways. However, when it reached Lake Van the mountains presented an almost impenetrable barrier to all but travellers on foot by camel or horseback; so steep in fact that the engineers decided to install a train ferry when the railway was first planned as being cheaper than a tunnel through the mountains.

So with relief we went on our way to Van and it's castle protecting travellers on this dangerous section of highway. This was the area I mentioned earlier

Eyeball to Eyeball

Seljuk Bridge

which had been inhabited by Armenians that has since been made available to the Kurds.

The roads around Van were dangerous for another reason; they were subject to avalanches in winter. On another occasion we rounded a corner of the road only to be confronted by a sea of mud and refuse which completely blocked our way. A solitary old man and three children were standing gazing at the scene.

I went up to them to ask if they were alright and where were they living? Were they being looked after? and so forth. They assured us they were being looked after by the people in the next village. All their own family had been wiped out and the children were orphaned, but the sense of responsibility in the countryside was so strong that, with the help of Allah, they were confident that they would be protected. The philosophic reaction to calamity was impressive and moving.

One of the most interesting features on this road to the east was the original fortress of the Hittites at Bogazkale or Hattusas pronounced Boaz Kaly about 100 km from Ankara. It has only been made accessible in recent years but the discoveries made are remarkable. Any ruins which have survived for as long as 3,000 years with carvings in such excellent condition must be worth visiting but when the excavations made in recent years also reveal a people of great maturity and wisdom one wonders how we can consider ourselves civilised in comparison. Their sculptures rival those of the ancient Egyptian, as do their patterns of law and morality. But it is not the purpose of this book to become a guide.

Aegea, Roman Amphitheatre

Aegea, The Mediterranean Coastline

CHAPTER 15

Patricia's Diary

FOUR DAY TOUR OF AEGEA, WESTERN TURKEY

November 13th–17th 1964

We set off on the morning of Friday 13th on our way to Denizli where Tom was to attend the tail-end of a seminar on Community Development, together with a Turkish Colleague - Aslan Bey. It was a gorgeous day, and we were all pleased to get away from Ankara for a change. Our first stop was at Afyon, where we had a very good lunch, starting with tripe soup, of which one gets quite fond in time. Then we had a walk round the bazaars, which were straight out of the middle ages. The whole town is dominated by a rocky fortress on top of a hill, which looks quite unassailable from one side, though doubtless there is a way in round the back. We saw too a superb memorial to the fallen in the war against Greece, the final battle having been fought quite near here in 1923, when the Greeks were finally driven back to the sea by Ataturk and his army. After lunch we carried on till we got to Denizli, over an atrocious road which is newly built, but will be very good, possibly next year. At Denizli we had to make enquiries at the police station as to where the rest of the "group" were staying, and in a short time had tracked them down and booked ourselves in at the same place. It was a brand new hotel only open a week, and even had a washbasin in the room AND a plug in it. The only snag was that the door had a huge glass panel in it with a light on all night shining into ones eyes. However I sneaked out in the middle of the night and turned it off and when I got back again Tom woke up and thought I was a marauder. However, we slept well for the rest of the night.

Next day, Saturday, after a hurried hot-milk-and-borek breakfast in the town, Tom and Aslan went off to the seminar. I strolled round the town but it is rather modern and uninteresting, having been entirely destroyed by an earthquake at the beginning of the century and recently rebuilt. They all came back at lunch time, and we set off straight away for a spot called Pamukkale - Cotton Castle - 30 kms away, as it was looking black and thundery and we didn't want to waste time. There are hot springs at Pamukkale which cascade over a kind of

Eyeball to Eyeball

Kursadasi

cliff, so that the entire hillside looks like a frozen waterfall. It also looks like piles of cotton wool. The springs flow down to the valley in a number of channels, and everything has turned white - grass, bushes etc. At the two hotels they have been enclosed in bathing pools and are supposed to be good for rheumatism, but it was too cold for anyone to want to strip their clothes off when we were there, though the water would have been a pleasant temperature. The ancient city of Hieropolis is in the same area.

After lunch at one of the hotels, we headed back to the west again, and drove to the coast, mostly through terrific rain, thunder and lightening. We found a small hotel in a fishing village, Kursadasi, which was quite adequate. Luckily next morning was fine and sunny, and the sea looked blue and inviting. Various Greek islands are only a few miles away, Samos and Chios, and further on Lesbos. We found a lovely camping spot in an olive grove on the edge of the sea, which we thought would do very nicely. We explored the considerable ruins of Ephesus and wished we had longer to spend there. There is a mile long Marble Way down to the old port, with columns on each side, also an amphitheatre which is being excavated now, and numerous other temples and gymnasia. In the museum we saw the famous statue of Diana which was nearly perfect. We dragged ourselves away from all this rather reluctantly, and went on to Ismir, about 30 miles on. There we just drove through the town and had

Patricia's Diary

a walk along the quay, but it was too early for lunch and so we went on. While passing through a small town 20 kms on Aslan Bay asked us to stop as he had two friends there, one the Kaymakam (or District Commissioner) and the other the Public Prosecutor. So we stopped in the main street while he went and made enquiries. Eventually they both met us at the Town Kulubu for a glass of tea. A joyous reunion ensued, as they hadn't seen each other for about 5 years, and had originally been friends at the University, they had lots of news to exchange. They then invited us all to lunch with them at a little place farther up the coast. We had to have lunch somewhere, and it was on our way, so we accepted. They all piled into the back of our car, the Kaymakam's car being hors de combat in some way, and drove on for about 20 kms till we reached a small seaside village with two lokantas right on the edge of the sea. They were both rather crowded, but there were some fresh fish available for us, so we strolled along the small jetty while we waited for it to be caught (I suspect), cleaned and cooked. When it did come at last it was extremely good, and we had a huge fish each, overlapping the plate by several inches on both sides. It was a fish exclusive to the Aegean Sea called Cippora. After everything had been eaten and two bottles of raki consumed (but not by Tom and me) we felt we had to carry on with our journey. The Kaymakam and Public Prosecutor did their best to persuade Aslan to stay the night and fly next day from Izmir, but he finally decided reluctantly to go on with us. By the time we left, the sun was getting low. We drove on round the coast and through various fishing ports, pausing now and then for Aslan to try to buy a tin of olive oil for his wife, as it is much cheaper and better here apparently. However, as he was a "tourist" the shopkeepers asked a price that was the same as in Ankara, so he didn't buy any. It was dark by five, but too early to stop, so we turned inland, and our last 80 miles was over a very mountainous bit in the dark, which was a pity. Eventually, we got to the small town of Balikesar, and found a hotel. Aslan retired to bed immediately, as he had had more lunch (and raki) than we had, but we had a snack and soup before turning in. Our room wasn't at all bad, but the washing arrangements are always a bit awkward in these small places. The only washbasin was in the passage, so one couldn't do much washing, and it was anyway rather draughty. Aslan had a wretched night as apparently the night porter slept in the other bed in his room and was continually going in and out. We had three beds in ours, but mercifully no one was put in with us, or we should have had something to say. We were charged for two beds too, contrary to custom.

Next day, Monday, we tried to make an early start, but there was such thick fog everywhere, that progress was slow. We had a delicious breakfast in a breakfast shop near the hotel, consisting of bread and thick honey and cream, with tea. The cream, I have since discovered, comes from buffalo milk, which doesn't sound very appetising, but it was very good when one didn't know its origin.

Eyeball to Eyeball

Glades near Bursa

After half an hour when we had got on to higher ground the fog lifted. We went through quite interesting country, along river valleys till we got near the sea again, when the principal crop seems to be sugar beet. We wanted to have a look at the Sea of Marmara, so did a quick, detour of the port of the Bandemir, and on to the seaside resort of Erdek. The latter was nice now, but in summer I am sure, would be a seething mass of tourists and campers from Bursa and Istanbul. We retraced our steps, and at length, reached Bursa. It was noon, later than we had intended, and we still had a long way to Ankara, so we had to choose a very few sights to see. Aslan only wanted to try the famous Iskender Kebab, apparently known all over Turkey, but we insisted on seeing the Green Mosque first, and very beautiful it was too; the interior covered in turquoise tiles and mosaic patterns. Behind was the tomb of Sultan Mehmet and all his relations, including his nanny, but it was closed, so we could only admire the outside which was very striking, a round sort of dome, covered all over by greenyblue tiles. After this, we succumbed to Aslan's pleas for sustenance, and tracked down the famous lokanta where the Iskender Kebab is to be found. We had to wait at least half an hour, but it was very good. The meat is somehow incorporated together into a huge wodge several feet long and a good 9 inches thick, which is grilled in front of charcoal on a vertical spit and then small thin pieces are sliced off and put on your plate, together with a few green peppers (the long hot kind), tomatoes, and yoghurt. If one is not quick enough to stop him, the waiter comes along with a saucepan full of sizzling melted fat which he pours over the whole thing, which makes it extremely indigestible. After this feast, we felt disinclined for much effort, but as Aslan was evidently dying to see the funicular railway which goes up the mountain behind the town, called Uludag, we agreed to go to the bottom and see where it starts from. As it happened, the cable car had just arrived, and was collecting passengers to go up again, but we decided it would take much too long, and in any case it was very cloudy and about to rain and the view would be nil. The cable car goes up to two stations, and at the second one there is a famous resort with good skiing in winter, and Alpine scenery, which we would love to go to some time.

We left about three, and then had to spend some time hunting for chestnuts which Aslan Bey said were a speciality of the Bursa district, and at about the fourth shop he found some good ones and bought a kilo to take back. We bought some eggs and bread and tangerines to take home, the eggs subsequently turning out to be all bad.

Bursa is in a very fertile area, with orchards everywhere, and I believe people flock to see it in spring time when the blossom is out. It was very beautiful and quite unlike any other part of Turkey that we had seen. As we were passing through one district, that of Bilecik, Tom remembered he had visited it earlier in the summer, and he wanted Aslan to see a certain village who had achieved a great deal by community development methods, with no government help whatsoever. They had built half a mile of road to the main road, added a room to the school, built a guest house and office for the Muhtar planted trees all along the road, and an orchard and park behind the village. So we turned off and drove up the new road to the village. The Muhtar was away, but everyone was very glad to see us and remembered Tom's previous visit. We were ushered into their smoky little tea house, and given glasses of tea while they discussed their problems with Aslan and Tom. They implored us to stay for supper and the night, but we had to go on. As we were leaving we had a few words with the school teachers, two young girls in ordinary modern dresses who must feel rather lonely in a small village like that miles from anywhere where all the women were swathed in veils and wore baggy trousers, and were kept strictly in their place. But they looked very cheerful and seemed to enjoy their work.

After that it was pitch dark, so we carried on till we got home, after about 3 hours driving. As we passed through the town of Eskisehir, Aslan murmured that it was famous for meerschaum, and would we like to stop and see some, but we managed to get out of that. Our only last contretemps was that when we got home, Tom found he had been wearing his reading glasses instead of his long distance ones. He only wears them for driving at night, and I had handed

Eyeball to Eyeball

him the ones I had in my bag, not knowing that he had two pairs. He said he wondered why all the lights flickered like stars, and I wondered why we sometimes went so close to oncoming traffic - but however, alls well that ends well.

The car went very well on that journey, about 1200 miles, and we only had one puncture. Admittedly the roads were mostly tarred, but it was quite a good performance. We boiled going up a steep mountain near Ephesus, but that was because it was warm weather and we had antifreeze in the radiator.

CHAPTER 16

Whirling Dervishes

BY PATRICIA

Caravanserai near Konya

For the first fortnight in December, the death of the poet and mystic, Mevlana, is commemorated in Konya. He lived in the 13th century, and founded an Islamic sect called the Whirling Dervishes. This sect was suppressed by Ataturk, but permission was granted for the celebrations for two weeks a year only.

So, on Sunday the 5th December, we set off with a coach load of tourists, to see what went on, knowing very little about what we were going to see. There were three coach-loads, the majority of passengers being Turks, many of them family parties comprising father, mother and several children, plus grannies and aunts as well. We left at 8, and bowled off to Konya. Our seats were well

Eyeball to Eyeball

back in the bus, and it was a most restful mode of travel compared to driving one's own car. One couldn't see traffic approaching, so did not witness any narrow squeaks which occurred, the inevitable consequence of any road travel in Turkey. On one occasion, going up a hill, a bus behind tried to pass, and we were racing two abreast most of the way up the hill, but we managed to pull away, and fortunately nothing was coming in the other direction. After an hour we reached the fork in the road where the main road goes on to Adana and the south, while we turned right to Konya. We had a few minutes halt at the cafe there, just time for some tea. Then on to Konya, which took another 2 1/2 hours, during most of which I slept soundly, there being little of interest at the best of times on that excessively boring road over the Anatolian plain. We arrived at about 12, and were taken up to a large Merchant's Club on a slight rise overlooking the town, where there was a huge dining hall laid out with long tables. Here we had a rather inferior lunch which took about an hour and a half. But we were not in any hurry so what did it matter. The lunch was included in our ticket, and we were allowed to choose from three groups, the first either biber dolmas (stuffed green pepper) or patlican isgara (fried egg plant, with or without yoghurt). Of course, on choosing the stuffed pepper, we were told it was "off" and we could have stuffed cabbage leaves instead, which we did (quite revolting and stone cold). Next came sis kebab or sis kofte, and the latter wasn't too bad, but not much of it. To follow, one could have plain yoghurt, compote which was mostly juice with a few slices of stewed fruit lying drowned at the bottom, or fresh fruit. To our surprise we were then offered some more stuffed cabbage leaves, which we declined. All this was to the accompaniment of a three piece band with piano, accordion and drums, all played by the most lugubrious men I have ever seen. They started off with the Merry Widow Waltz, and Colonel Bogey, and continued with other Palm Court selections, and cheered up quite a bit by the time they had finished.

After this feast, I had a 20 minute wait queuing for the "Ladies" which, as there was no water whatever, was a somewhat sordid experience. Once more we climbed into our buses, and set off on a tour of the town, though in fact we drove in a dead straight line for about 5 miles, and then turned round, and we were told that we should have got out and walked round some "Military Park", but as it was raining by that time, this part of the programme was left out. We then reached the "Stadium" where the celebrations were going to take place. We were rather taken aback to see a large open air football stadium in front of us, which would have been chilly and wet in the extreme, but fortunately our goal was instead a basket ball stadium, under cover. This had a shiny wooden floor, and we all sat on two sides of the hall on wooden benches, softened by cushions hired at 50 kurush apiece. The hall was packed. At one end was a raised dais, with a painted backcloth depicting the Mevlana Monastery and

Whirling Dervishes

minaret, and at the other end was a huge picture of the poet himself surrounded by Turkish flags. A few rows of chairs for VIPs were in front of this.

At 2.30, a man appeared from a door at the far end, climbed on to the dais, and gave a speech, which was greeted by much applause, though we could not understand anything. This was followed by about an hour of poetry readings, and solos on a sort of bamboo pipe, given by various gentlemen in city suits. We were sitting in the front row, so one could lean forward and almost doze off, as it was all rather soporific. At last, all this stopped, and a 15 minute interval was announced. So we got up and went into the main entrance hall which was lined with stalls selling all the most frightful tourist trash one could imagine, which however were going like hot cakes. We bought a few postcards and consumed some gazoz (fizzy drinks), and returned to our seats.

About 15 men appeared, dressed in long robes covered with black cloaks, wearing tall fezes, and mounted the dais. This was the orchestra, and they sat on the floor. Then the dervishes appeared, wearing the same garments, and lined up on one side of the room. The head dervish, evidently very holy and respected wore the same clothes, but his tall fez had a border of black fur at the bottom. They all bowed low to each other, and then the head priest on the dais began to intone a long chant about the poet Mevlana and at the very holy bits everyone bowed low again. The dervishes then began to process very slowly round the room, with the head priest in the lead. At one end of the room one would turn round and bow low to the next man, and this would be repeated as each man got to the spot. They went round three times, everything being done very slowly and deliberately, the orchestra playing a haunting tune meanwhile. They all lined up again. The head priest stood on his prayer mat at the far end of the room. The dervishes then approached him one by one, having thrown off their cloaks first, then with their hands crossed and placed on each shoulder, they bowed to him, and then began to twirl. Gradually, their hands would be unfolded, they stretched out their arms, and twirled round and round, their skirts which were circular, flaring out about them. Their robes were mostly white, and they wore a short white jacket on top, with one side fastened with a string, and the other flapping loose. One man was in dark green, and one man and a small boy were in light green and one in crimson, but we did not discover the significance of this. At last they were all whirling round and round, never touching each other, and apparently oblivious of everything. Some had their heads on one side, but all their arms were outstretched the palm of one hand pointing up to heaven and the other down to the ground. After about 10 minutes there must have been some sign as they all stopped dead, and shuffled backwards till they were on the edge of the floor in groups of two and three. They never staggered or appeared in the least dizzy. Then they walked slowly

Eyeball to Eyeball

round till they were in a long straight line again, and it all began again. One by one they approached the chief priest, bowed low, and began to twirl. Meanwhile he stood on his prayer mat quite still, and two other dervishes still in their black cloaks watched the whirlers closely, why I do not know. This went on for about an hour, and it was indeed a strange sight. They must go into a sort of trance of religious ecstasy. Then the music stopped. They all backed to the side of the room, and one of the onlooking dervishes, as they knelt down, placed their cloaks round their shoulder again. The chief dervish knelt down, bowed with his forehead against the floor, and said something I presume in Arabic, as the only things I could understand was "salaam aleikum" and then he let out an unearthly howl, which all the others joined it. He then slowly and with their particular hesitating step, one step and then wait, then another step and wait, and so on, till he got to the far end where the orchestra were, turned and bowed, and then walked out. Each one turned and bowed in the same spot, and they all went out. And that was the end.

We came out into the entrance hall, which was a milling mass of people buying curios, drinks, sweets, and buns, and saw a few people we knew (Walter, Rizve etc.) and eventually joined our buses once more. We then were taken to what is known as the Mevlana Museum, or Convent of the Whirling Dervishes. It was a "convent" or rather a monastery founded by Mevlana, and he and his numerous relations are buried there. By this time it was 4.30 and pitch dark. The museum was shut, but was eventually opened while we stood around in a thin drizzle. We went into the inner courtyard, and approached the inner building, where we had to remove our shoes and put on special slippers. Then we filed in past all the tombs, rows of them. Their coffins are rounded on the top, sometimes made of mosaics or marble, and covered with various embroidered cloths, and at their head is a huge twisted white turban with a dark cone shaped cylinder sticking up through the middle. The holier the man the higher the turban. Mevlana's tomb must be a very holy and revered spot, as I noticed all the women approaching with their hands out, palms upwards, sighing and groaning and some in tears. (A friend told us when she was there last year, a woman had a sort of fit and fell rigid to the ground. She was rather concerned, being a nurse, thinking it was epilepsy, and all ready to render first aid, but the woman's husband told her not to worry, she was only in a trance, overcome by the extreme holiness of her surroundings). There were many beautifully illuminated Korans, and koran stands, ornamental mosque lamps and musical instruments in glass cases, and a few cases containing Mevlana's clothing, which seemed to be in a remarkable state of preservation. We had just come to the end of the exhibits, and were standing in front of a glass case containing a beautiful inlaid box, and I had just read out the notice that it contained the beard of, possibly Mevlana, or could it have been Mohamed,

Whirling Dervishes

when the lights fused and we were plunged in total darkness. We waited what seemed to be several minutes and as no one produced a light Tom thought we had better try to get out, so lit a match to see what direction to proceed in. Frightful consternation. A museum official was standing in front of the box with the Beard, with arms outstretched in front of it, thinking no doubt that we were about to try and make off with it, and T. was told on no account to light matches and certainly not to throw the end on the floor. So we remained motionless in the dark for another few minutes, till a candle was brought, and we were all shepherded out as fast as possible. Finding our shoes was quite a feat, and then with some difficulty we emerged and found our bus among a good many others. The whole town was in darkness, so there was no point in our wandering about window shopping till the bus went in half an hour, so we stayed in our seats, and eventually tea was brought from a nearby tea shop, and very welcome too. Suddenly the town was lit up again, but as there was only 5 minutes before we were due to go, we stayed where we were.

Everyone was collected, and off we went again. After about an hour we stopped and the driver muttered something about a broken petrol pipe, and I had visions of our spending the night on the road. However, he managed to repair it, and we got as far as the turn off where we had stopped before, where we had a 25 minute break. By this time it was after eight, so we had a meal. The cafe is so used to buses disgorging passengers there and stopping for short periods that they produce food in minutes. We had a kind of roast beef, which was very good. Finally we piled in for the last time, and reached Ankara with no further mishaps, about 10.30. Most of the children had sunk into exhausted slumber by this time, and were either roused or carried out by father wrapped in shawls. We found our car still intact by the office of the tourist agency, and went home. A very interesting day, and we wouldn't have missed it for anything.

CHAPTER 17

On the Hippy Trail

BY PATRICIA

ANATOLIA

Uneventful journey. The last time I was on that road was with the Dunings I think, in a minibus with a dreadful driver. Then we also traversed that road with the Noad family Dorothy, Jos, Andrew and Priscilla two years ago when we stayed at Unye. Now the road has been much improved, in fact a new one constructed, and it is mostly very good. I always enjoy that drive and the country rather than that boring 3 hour stretch across the Anatolian plain. Stopped a few minutes in Corum for T. to tinker with the engine. A crowd collected in no time, with helpful suggestions and even outstretched arms to help tinker too. It was a glorious day, warm and just like summer, and not so dry as the atmosphere in Ankara. Gorgeous to get away - I felt better at once. Unye looked exactly the same, but the Piknik kiosk where we used to go down to bathe has disappeared. We decided to get to Ordu, and should have got in in daylight but there was a large stretch of wet tar so we had to crawl along to avoid being splattered. No gravel had been put on top of course.

Stayed at Turistik Otel, apparently quite new, obliging staff. We had a room with a cold shower, which was refreshing but with the usual awkward fittings. The shower water descended straight onto the loo seat, or if twizzled round, it went all over the rest of the room and even outside the door into the passageway. To clean ones teeth was equally hazardous. The taps jutted out so far that it was quite difficult to aim into the extra small basin, and if one bent right down one was in danger of cutting one's forehead open on the edge of the glass shelf above it. I was bitten to hosts by mosquitoes in the night and of course the flit was down in the car. Also I was kept awake by heavy traffic roaring through on the straight coast road outside.

Oct. 6 Thursday. Left after breakfast outside on the terrace. Delightful drive along the coast, perfect day with the sea and sky as blue as the Mediterranean. Stopped to take a photo at Giresun which seemed a pretty little port, with a

Eyeball to Eyeball

peninsular jutting out and the town on both sides of it. A cruise ship, the Marmara, was in port. We got to Trabzon after lunch, which we ate in a delightful site overlooking the sea, on an old piece of road but out of sight of the new with green grass and wild flowers all round. Looked round for an hotel, all of them looked pretty crummy. Chose the Konak Palas as it looked new and some of the grubu had stayed there last time T. was through. It was nice and clean, but the chief snag was that it was on the road up from the port, and a one way street at night for all the through traffic. As it was also on a steepish hill all the lorries ground their way up making a terrific almost unbearable din and one could hardly hear oneself think. At night the neon sign outside lit up the room with a bright red and green light, so we had to draw the curtains and shut the door to the balcony to keep out as much noise as possible. Otherwise it wasn't too bad. One lot of guests next door left in the middle of the night making the maximum of noise, and the muezzin started yelling at about 4.30 a.m., but otherwise we had a good night. However, we decided that one night was enough, so checked out. In the afternoon after our arrival we had found our way to the Agaia Sofian, an old Byzantine church now a museum. It had been restored by some people from Edinburgh museum, and the murals were interesting and the church in good shape. But no notice directing one there or anything. The man in charge pointed out Ataturk's "palace" on the top of the hill and said we ought to go there as it was far more interesting. So up we went, up Cold Water Hill (Soguk Su). Found the Kiosk, just like a wedding cake with the icing dripping down the sides. In v. good repair and well maintained and everything in the very worst of taste. I think I have never seen such hideous furniture and fittings, except perhaps in Ataturk's summer house in Ankara. Terrible lamps, though the one in the main hall was not bad in a striking way, huge blue glass bowl surrounded by dangling glass things. Upstairs wonderful view over the pine woods to the sea and town. The garden was lush with roses and hideous tassels of purple Love-lies-Bleeding which we both loathe. Descended the hill and drove round the town which is not as romantic as Rose Macaulay depicts. Had dinner at Emperyal restaurant, which wasn't bad, but lights too dim so one couldn't see what one was eating. Walked round the town afterwards and found by chance the famed silver market, which didn't look up to much or worth another visit.

Friday. Left to go to Mereyamana Monastery. Really beautiful drive up the valley with towering mountains on each side. Very like Switzerland or Austria. At a village of Macka we turned off on to the forest track, which no one had warned me about and I was petrified. About 10 miles of narrow track climbing 2000 feet or so, with fearful precipices on one side. If one had met anything I don't know what we should have done. T. took it all very calmly as he had done it before and seemed surprised at my apprehension. The Peugeot didn't turn a hair. When we got to the Forest station, it was all much as I had imagined it, only more magnificent if possible. The monastery towers above one and is hollowed out of cliffs and at first you don't see it, as it is so far above one. We drove past the Forest station so as to get a photograph slightly from the side. Left the car and climbed up a twisting track, 1000 feet to the monastery. Much to our fury we found the door, the one and only door, was firmly locked. So Tom went down another track to find a key, leaving me sitting on a seat a little way down. I wrote post cards to the children to while away the time and read the Blue Guide, and he was back in about half an hour, having run down and ascended at once. He came armed with the most enormous key about 9 inches long. There was no one in charge, and a Forester at the bottom has tried to say that a) the door was not locked and b) there was a guard there anyway, neither of which statements were true. So up we trundled again, climbed the steep stairs with frightful drop on one side, and inserted the key in the lock. But try as we might it would not turn, and in fact we had great difficulty in getting it out again. We tried everything, or rather T. did, hammering it with stones and rocks and using a branch of a tree as a lever all to no avail. If we had had an iron bar with which to break down the door we should have done so, we were so infuriated. But finally we had to go away having only seen the outside. There is no other way in as it is built more or less flush with the rocky cliff face and the other side is even more precipitous. Outside is an old aqueduct half falling down. We took a few photos, and then the sun went in and the clouds began to come down over the mountain tops. But the slopes were so beautiful with the trees - beeches and birches and oaks all turning gold and orange and red, interspersed with the huge pine trees. The Forest Station is at 3000 feet and the monastery about 1000 feet higher. Back to the car we went. Everywhere there were fungi growing, pushing through the tree roots and lush underground, some of them the most gorgeous orange with yellow spots like the fairy tales. Everything was lush and damp, and a river rushing through and down the rocks at the bottom. We handed in the key as we went past with many despairing noises at our non success. One oaf offered to come with us again and have a try, but we didn't think he would be more successful than we had been as he had no official status anyway, and the door had probably been locked for some time as there are not many visitors at this time of year. Anyway T. had had two trips and it was clouding over so we didn't think it was worth it. At any rate, for me the trip had been worthwhile even just seeing the outside of the monastery. That was probably better than the inside, but I was sorry not to have seen where the boys had laboured at their work camp in August. T. showed me the cave where they had had their camp fires and where they slept. The boards on which they had slept were in the cave so someone else had presumably used them too. There were flowers everywhere just like spring, huge mauve crocuses, and then blackberries and spindle berries too.

Eyeball to Eyeball

When we got back to the main road again we turned left and drove up the Erzerum road towards the Zigana Pass - 6000 feet. But we only got to about 4000 feet and the clouds were coming so low down that we couldn't see any view, so decided to turn. The trees were marvellous colours. Stopped in Macka to try and find a map of the district and some aprons made of striped red and whitish pink shuka stuff, also one of the woven bands which the boys bought as ties but I shall use as a belt. Posted pcs but goodness knows when they will arrive at home. Back in Trabzon we booked in at the Benli Palas hotel which looked very modern from the outside, but not so once one had got inside. Still it wasn't at all bad. We had a so-called shower. This proved not very effective, the water squirted from every joint both upwards and downwards in every direction, but most of the water was coming from half way up so was not of much use. There was the typical ottoman washing bowl made of marble also a marble block to sit on. The technique is to sit on the block and scoop water over yourself with a kind of brass jellymould. The snag is that the marble basin has no outlet hole so swiftly gets filled with scummy water that is impossible to get rid of. Seems a very one-horse arrangement as surely a hole with a pipe connected to the drain would not be very difficult to devise. The Romans had drain pipes so why not the modern Turks? Luckily we didn't have a loo, as they all smelled atrocious, the reason being that the flushing arrangements had been broken so no water went down except that which you poured with the aid of a small tin mug.

We had supper at the Imren lokanta, one of those very rapid service places which cater for bus passengers. The result is that if you are not careful you find you have been served with and have consumed a three course meal in about half an hour and then have to find a way of passing the evening. This happened to be a "dry" lokanta, and seemingly only forks and spoons allowed, no knives, but don't know if there is any connection. Four little partridges were running about the floor picking up crumbs from under the tables. Occasionally one would see them wanting to go to sleep and trying to find some shade from the glare of the neon lights under a chair or against the wall. Their eyes would close, their feathers would fluff up and they would have a few minutes snooze, then wake up refreshed to pursue the crumbs once more.

Saturday. Quite a good night. Our room looked out over the harbour over a roof of rather nice pantiles, but slightly marred by all the rubbish thrown out - apple peel, cigarette ends and paper. We had to put the car in a sort of repair yard in front of the hotel, as it had no approach road at all, just a narrow lane entirely filled by a large American taxi. The repair yard people were very helpful and nice, but the whole place was inches thick in oil and grease so that every step caked ones shoes in oily mud. But there was nowhere else to put it.

On the Hippy Trail

We left about 8, but stopped on the way out to buy a pes tamal to make a shirt for Mike. Tried a draper, and were directed to the bazaar which we had not previously seen. It proved to be a fascinating place, better than Ankara, and most colourful with the shops full of cloths and luminous jerseys and wool, and the different wood and copper craftsmen. Bought just what I wanted and a few embroidered tablecloths. Then we walked down to see what the sea front looked like. It may be very magnificent one day as a new road is being built round the sea edge. But now it is terribly sordid. A new piece of tarmac has evidently been used as a slaughter house judging by the pools of blood, skulls, bones and teeth lying about, and it has been built on land reclaimed by the piling up of rubbish. A sewer runs straight out into the sea with a nasty smell and appearance, and altogether a lot will need doing to it, as the buildings are all antiques. I wanted very much to buy a new wooden cradle which I thought would do to put magazines in, but reason prevailed as it was so large, and I suppose it would be rather a shame to use it for such a purpose. But they were nice.

Back to the car. Rather a dull day and had rained along the road. We nearly got stuck in a patch which was being done up before Giresun. One heavily loaded lorry did get stuck and had to be dragged out by a bull dozer, which of course did not go back and smooth over the ruts. However the Peugeot proved reliable again and we did not have any trouble. Had lunch by the sea and T. changed a wheel as there appeared to be a slow puncture. Stopped in at Ordu as T. had left his reading glasses there and luckily they had been handed in by the cleaning woman. Got to Samsun as it was getting dark, rather dangerous with all the unlighted carts and cattle on the road. Booked in at the Turistik Otel Vidinli where we had stayed before. Seems to have improved. We actually had a bathroom with a full size bath, a loo with plumbing that worked, no smell, bath mats, towels, the lot. Judging by the literally scores of pipes the central heating was an afterthought, but we had no complaints otherwise.

Next day after breakfast we thought we had better have the spare wheel mended so that took half an hour, while we read last week's Sunday Times.

Lovely day, particularly when we got inland. We went via Amasra, a most intriguing old place, deep in the bottom of a rocky valley with huge rocky mountains on each side, dominated by an ancient castle on the highest peak. The river Yesilirmak ran along the valley and the town was built on both sides of it. Some of the cliffs had rock tombs carved in the sides. Took my last remaining photos, bought some fruit and back to the main road again. We passed all sorts of villages with stations, with literally hundreds of carts and lorries all queuing up filled with sugar beet. They must have had to wait all day,

Eyeball to Eyeball

as there only seemed to be four or five trucks at the most being loaded. But the Turk is admirably suited to waiting. No one can look so comfortable asleep on a load of sugar beet, or logs, or even concrete blocks, as they can.

Had another puncture beyond Corum, due, we later discovered, to the inferior glue used when patching inner tubes. We were watched by four ragged little boys who said not a word but took the greatest interest. On our departure I could not think of anything to give them, so offered a bit of Sunday Times. They immediately became like ravening wolves, fighting each other over the pages, so I handed over the whole paper, including the colour supplement. We left them wrestling over the remnants. We had the tyre mended at Sungurlu and a new tube put in for safety's sake.

Owing to the various delays we didn't get in to Ankara till dusk and had been travelling all the afternoon straight into the setting sun, and a glorious orange sunset. It seemed to be even worse bedlam than usual. Cars and lorries approaching, sometimes coming the wrong way down a two lane road and cutting across one's bows, quite often with two red lights in front and one white one behind, or else green and red and blue all round the front and nothing at all in the rear. Pedestrians dash across the roads everywhere without looking first to see what is coming, with a touching faith that they can be clearly seen by the approaching motorist, dolmuses stopping suddenly in the middle of the road to discharge passengers, who then dart across in front of the car, cows trooping off home and wandering across as fancy leads them, horses and carts with no lights of any kind and no rules of the road - usually they face the oncoming traffic on the wrong side of the road. In fact, we heaved a sigh of relief at getting home without hitting anything. 1116 miles in all in 5 days.

ANTIOCH

TAURUS MOUNTAINS

We visited Antakya one June. Antakya is the old Anticoh in Pisidia visited by St. Paul and St. Peter, and one of the earliest churches. I have found it fascinating each time we have been there. It has an atmosphere all its own. You come over the mountains from Iskenderun down into the valley of the Orontes and there is Antakya at the foot of another range of mountains. A wall from Roman times can be seen running along the top where the old citadel was, and half way down can be seen the old aqueduct, coming from miles away, and half dug into the rock so that at intervals it disappears completely. We followed it one evening and found that it evidently had ended in a colossal dam right across a valley, a considerable feat in those days.

On the Hippy Trail

The Taurus Mountains

Antakya has an authentic Middle Eastern flavour. It used to be part of Syria when it was handed over to Turkey. In modern Syrian maps it is still marked as belonging to Syria, although the actual border now is a good 30 miles away. On entering the town you come to a huge roundabout and then a wide bridge over the Orontes, a rather muddy looking flow of water but quite impressive. On the far side of the bridge you come to the hub of the old town and the beginning of the bazaar, which we found to be as fascinating as any we had come across in Turkey. At the end of the bridge stand a couple of sellers of what we thought to be lemonade, their twinkling brass containers slung on their backs, a bandolier with glasses slung round the waist so that the stuff could be poured out with the minimum of trouble. It seemed a popular beverage and we thought we would sample some while trying to get a photograph. It looked like cold tea and tasted bitter and the vendor did not want to be photographed but we managed to get a not very good picture. Nearby was a long row of shoe cleaners sitting on stools with their highly polished brass apparatus containing various kinds and colours of polish and usually a picture of some romantic scene or bathing beauty on the front.

There were six of us in our party, my husband who was on official business, my daughter and a friend, my stepmother and brother who was on his way to Syria and Jordan. One morning we were wandering round the bazaar and saw

Eyeball to Eyeball

some very pretty material, which my stepmother thought would be ideal for a button through cotton skirt. She really needed one for this trip so we decided to get it made up by one of the many "ladies tailors" which seemed to abound. One after another shook their heads or at least did the Turkish equivalent, which is to throw the head back, close the eyes and smile sweetly, which we soon got to realise meant no. At length a small boy of about 10 said he would lead us to someone. We followed him for half a mile, through alleyways, up and down steps, across court-yards, till we were beginning to suspect he was leading us "up the garden path", till eventually he dived into a doorway in a wall and we found ourselves in an enclosed court-yard with rooms all round off it and found that the owner did dressmaking. It then dawned on us that these ladies tailors only made outside garments like coats, and nothing below the waist in any case. With the aid of a dictionary and many signs we managed to convey to the lady of the house what we wanted, the material was displayed and measurements taken, and we were bidden to return at 8 o'clock that evening. Hoping that we would be able to find our way again through the labyrinthine lanes we thanked her and departed.

That evening on our way out to have supper, we again traversed those cobbled lanes and found ourselves outside the door in the wall, the right one we hoped. It was, and on ringing the bell, the door was flung open and when we entered, we found ourselves engulfed by the entire family, husbands, brothers, sons as well as grandmothers and daughters. We were ushered into an elaborately furnished sitting room and regaled with lemonade while conversation ensued in halting Turkish on the purpose of our visit, what we were doing in Turkey, and in return we were told that the family was not Turkish but Christian - Catholic, and most of the women seemed to be called Mary. The news that one of our party was also Mary was greeted with great enthusiasm, though unfortunately we didn't have any medallions to display from round our necks. We were beginning to wonder whether after all we could decently get away and to hope that the skirt was in fact ready, when my stepmother was beckoned from the room to try it on. It was a perfect fit, the equivalent of 15/- was produced and profound thanks on all sides, and we at last emerged with many invitations to return for a visit another day.

We were staying in the best hotel in the main street and had rooms on the top floor so that it was a little less noisy than it might have been. Even so, I have never experienced such bedlam as ensued every night. Our rooms looked out over the river and on the other side was an open air cinema and we could see the screen clearly. Somehow each night we came to be at roughly the same time and could see one episode in the dramatic story. A girl seemed to be about to suffer a fate worse than death on a sofa when the door would open and father appeared with every appearance of hostility. We never bothered to get farther in the story than this so never saw the end. The film went on till after mid-night with the sound so loud that I should have thought that those actually inside the cinema compound would have had their eardrums permanently shattered but somehow in spite of all the din we always slept soundly through it. In the mornings life would begin before it was light with lorries revving up, horses and carts jingling through the streets, and at first light the sound of marching feet, and the army would appear headed by officers on horseback, tramping through the town and out the other side on long route marches, singing at the tops of their voices. Some hours later they would tramp back again, not singing this time, and even the horses drooping a bit, and this was repeated every day. On the last day of our stay my brother took off on his hitch hike to the south, and we all saw him into a bus which was going to the frontier at Yayladag. The bus was supposed to leave at 6 but we couldn't see it actually leave as we were going out for the day on an official tour. In actual fact, it didn't leave till nearly midday, as it had to wait until it filled up with passengers and time didn't really matter to anyone.

As for the rest of us, after breakfast at the hotel, we joined the convoy of government vehicles outside, headed by the governor of the province in his Land Rover with flag flying and followed by sundry trucks, pickups and jeeps. We could not have gone in our own car in any case as the roads were far too rough in places.

The convoy set off, well spaced because of dust once we left the tarmac, up the mountain at the back of Antakya and along the top to a place where a village leaders camp was in progress. White bell tents were set in a circle round a flag staff with the scarlet Turkish flag flying jauntily in the breeze. Under some shady trees were rows of chairs and a blackboard, where the teaching was taking place. We all occupied some seats of honour facing the pupils and the governor gave a speech introducing the official visitors from Ankara. More speeches followed and some sensible comments from the village leaders themselves. They were evidently as keen as mustard and enjoying the discussions.

We moved on and left them to it. We visited several villages and saw various projects for village improvement that were being instituted. A new drinking fountain plus cattle trough at one place, a new public lavatory at another, some home economics classes and village industries at another, with carpentry and woodwork a useful skill. At every place we were offered refreshment, glasses of tea or coffee, ayran or lemonade. The governor said he never gave notice of his visits as he did not want the villagers to feel that they had to provide meals out of their meagre resources, Turkish hospitality being overwhelming

Eyeball to Eyeball

traditionally. However, word had spread by bush telegraph and in one place we were ushered up a ladder into what was evidently the main bedroom of a house. Several trestle tables had been put up covered with sheets of oilcloth and the tables were soon loaded with huge dishes of rice, hard-boiled eggs, salad, yoghurt, and long loaves of ekmek. We each had a spoon and plate and dipped at random into the nearest place. Very good it all was too, topped with glasses of ayran. I was glad to see that there was a great deal left over, so the many on lookers did not go short after we had left.

Our tour ended at sunset, by a cool green lake at the foot of the mountains, a few miles from the Syrian border, and we sipped our last glasses of tea sitting by the water's edge while the days' doings were discussed. We got back as it was getting dark, and all retired thankfully to bed, feeling that we could not face another mouthful of food or drink for days.

LONG TREK TO ASIA January 15th 1966

RETURN TO TURKEY

We got up fairly early today as the train to Manchester went at 10.7. Last minute instructions about the carnet, and fortunately the insurance cover note arrived so the form could be filled by Tom. Got to the station in good time and saw the train off. What a gorgeous day, crisp, sunny, clear and very cold. Our bird bath was frozen solid, but no ice on the roads as it was so dry. I wandered round Truro doing a bit of shopping, when I saw a crowd lining the street in front of the City Hall. It was the meet, two huntsmen in pink coats and a crowd of excited hounds swept into the square and halted outside the Red Lion. The hounds rushed about, spending pennies on all the shop fronts and wagging their tails at the spectators, and finally gathered round the MFH (I suppose that is what he was) barking wildly at him. Other ponies and riders and horses joined them till there was quite a crowd, a typically English scene, foreigners would say. Eventually a stout barmaid with crimson hair emerged from the hotel bearing a tray of steaming glasses of punch and they were all given a stirrup cup, including the Lady Mayor and Mayoress, two diminutive women with gold chains round their necks. The town hall clock struck eleven, and off they all went through the middle of the town, with the hunting horn being blown at full blast.

I eventually got back home at 12.30, had some lunch, and decided to neglect the chores and go out so as not to miss the sunshine. Luckily just as I was opening the front door, the telephone rang and there was Jos, and then Marcus, who had just got back from Austria. He seems to have had a great time, the only snag being a shortage of pocket money which cramped his style rather towards the end. If only the dear boy had written to us earlier we might have sent him some, but we only got a pc from him yesterday. He sounded tired, so is going to stay at the flat tonight and come down tomorrow.

I then walked round the creek and back, low tide and beautiful, wearing Jos's poshteen and my Turkish sheepskin hat for warmth. Called in on Christine Boret and had a cup of tea with her.

I must confess I rather have cold feet about our forthcoming journey. The pictures from France are fearsome, snow everywhere and it is bound to be much worse later on. I wonder what will come of the Manchester trip. What will we be doing a year from now? Will the Manchester job come to anything, will the DTC release Tom or give him a 6 month contract, will they pay our passages? I am not looking forward to the next few weeks, the packing up and icy journey and general uncertainty. But I must stop worrying, or I shall never sleep. We have been frightfully lucky up till now so why not in the future? If only I really felt well I don't think I should worry so much, but there is this horrid feeling of sickness most of the time and particularly in the early morning, which puts a brake on everything. I hope it is just over tiredness as all these doctors say, and I wish it did not take so long to clear up.

If only we hadn't agreed to go back to Turkey for another year how much better it would have been. I think we have made a mistake though it would have been hard from the financial point of view. But perhaps that is just my cautious nature. I am a bit sick of continually packing up and living a makeshift life, but on the other hand I should get equally tired of sticking in the same place for the rest of my life. One part of me wishes to stay put, get to know people, put down roots and really feel oneself a necessary part of the community. And I do wish darling Tom could have his hearts desire - a decent boat and time and leisure to enjoy it. Perhaps it won't be too late. I wish I wasn't so hopeless and enjoyed sailing more.

Well that's enough drivel for one day. I intend too keep this diary regularly for the next year.

January 26. Our last morning at Trenant was pretty hectic. We had done most of the packing the day before and all the luggage was piled up in the rumpus room with anything else we hopefully wanted to take with us and it looked a vast pile. However, due to skilful packing by Tom it all went in and we could even look out of the back window. A horrid wet gusty day it was. I gradually went through the house cleaning and throwing away and leaving it (I hoped) in

Eyeball to Eyeball

order, and pushing everything surplus into the dressing room. Hadn't time to go all through the inventory to see that all was as in the list or we should never have got away at all. About 1 we took the sheets and other cleaning over to the Craven Sykes. About 2.30 we had shut the front door (remembered the two camp chairs in the porch and pushed them in the boot), got to the duka to pay the bill and leave the key, and away to Truro. Here we had to wait an hour while Tom went to the labour exchange to draw his national assistance! I was just so whacked I sat in the car doing absolutely nothing. By four we were actually under weigh (or is it way) and off we went. Tom seemed fairly fresh considering and I gradually revived. We got to Honiton by about 7 and stayed in the New Dolphin Hotel, very nice old coaching inn, with good room and good dinner which we were much in need of.

Next morning we were off early, and got to Julia's at Itchen Abbas about 11.45 for a belated coffee and chat. Got to London by 3 and Tom went off to have his medical. I managed to get some American Express Travellers cheques and get some shopping done. Marcus and Jos came round and we had a revolting meal at the New Kentucky in the Earls Court Road, but otherwise a pleasant evening.

Sunday 30th. To Dover where we embarked about 10, having filled up with petrol and written a hasty note to Mrs Allsopp to ask if M could leave a week early or late as DTC won't pay fare for a holiday under 3 weeks. Calm crossing, and uncrowded. As it was Sunday we could not get car spares, so off we went, and got to Chalons sur Marne. Hotel Angleterre, undistinguished but comfortable. By chance found a super restaurant, I should think the best and had an excellent meal.

Monday 31st. Left by 8 but spent about one hour getting chains from the Peugeot agent. Rather a drizzly dull day. Tom got wet opening the boot at lunch time to get out plates etc. and after that developed a very stiff and painful back which got worse and worse. Stopped that night at a small village off the autobahn somewhere near Stuttgart. We happened to see the sign HOTEL from the road and luckily found a room. It turned out that the proprietor was an Englishman from Dorset who had married a German girl. Maps of Devon and Cornwall up on the wall. The waitress also turned out to be English and was going to do the job till she went to University in the autumn. Huge feather eiderdown affairs which swamped one. Quite comfortable.

Tuesday 1st. Fast trip along the autobahn mostly till we got to Salzburg. Very pretty through Bavaria. We went over a mountain pass which got snowier and snowier but none on the road. At the highest point there was thick fog and a large hotel with disconsolate skiers walking about as the snow was not thick enough for skiing. Down again on to the autobahn. We arrived about lunch time and tried to find a garage to do a 2,000 mile service on the car. Had a hamburger and beer at a snack bar at an AGIP station, which would not do the service. So we eventually found the Peugeot agents who agreed to do it right away. Meanwhile we wandered around the suburb, rather bleak and slushy. Later, we drove round and found a hotel in a main street. Quite all right, but terribly noisy as there were a lot of beer halls and restaurants in the street and people seemed to come and go all night. Neither of us slept much and Tom felt positively ill, probably that hamburger which was covered with raw onion, but he didn't let himself be sick as the loo was in a hot cubby hole next to the office where the night porter slumbered. The loo paper was squares of newspaper, extremely tough and even that ran out by morning. Anyway we both felt a bit piano next day.

Wednesday 2nd. Along the autobahn to Vienna, not very pleasant as it was so foggy. Thence to Graz, also foggy and our speed was limited. Tom was feeling so stiff by that time that we decided not to go via Budapest after all as it would have added distance and he was in no fit state to sight see. I drove quite a bit. Got to Graz in the dark and drove round and round looking vainly for a gasthaus or hotel and at last found one, which proved to be very good, on a corner but we had a back room which was quiet, and had quite a good meal.

Thursday 3rd. On to Yugoslav frontier. Thick fog and more snow as we progressed so it was very slow. Bypassed Zagreb. What we could see of the country was dull and monotonous but one had to concentrate chiefly on the road and pedestrians and horses and carts and bicyclists looming out of the fog in front of one. Spent the night at Slavonski Brod, a dreary dump seemingly covered in a film of coal dust. The hotel a typical state owned establishment, new and huge and the room well appointed but completely without character. We appeared to be the only guests. Had dinner in the restaurant, very dull, just scheinecotelets with nothing else to embellishment except a tomato each which looked as though embalmed and turned out to be sort of pickled with a liberal sprinkling of paprika. Quite a good cake though. There was a huge banqueting hall downstairs with an orchestra and the locals were coming in for drinks just as we were going to bed. We had our own bathroom and it was very comfortable and only about £1 each a night. On the door was a long list of rules, and more could apparently be obtained by applying to the desk. The tariff on the door included the use of the telephone (there wasn't one) about 3d, sojourn tax whatever that was 3d-6d, insurance about 1/2d and notification of stay about 2 1/2d. We thought the insurance might be necessary as there were huge cracks in the outside walls and holes dug in the bathroom walls and the whole place looked a bit flimsy.

Eyeball to Eyeball

Friday 4th. Left S.B. early and had quite a good drive to the Bulgarian frontier, country still monotonous, but it improved after Belgrade when the road was not so straight and the surface better. Belgrade had impressive new buildings but the old part looked murky and the streets were piled with dirty slush which got swished all over the car by passing trams. We did not stop. We reached the frontier just as it was getting dark. We had to wait a bit and have the car examined, afterwards we were told they were looking for people being smuggled in or out. On to Sofia, which we reached about 7. Went round and round looking for a hotel. T. went into a huge edifice called the Grand Hotel Balkan, and I sat in the car for about 3/4 of an hour. There was no room in any hotel so the Information Office had arranged a room for us in a private apartment in the suburbs. We had to leave the car in an enclosure in the centre of town, and go by car provided by the Information Office (at our expense) to the apartment which seemed miles away, but he pointed out the local sights as we went along. The block was a typically Turkish one, the flat was 5 floors up, and the light kept going off before we got up to the top. We were greeted by a young man son of the house, and shown our room which was a bedroom and dining sitting room divided by a curtain, crowded with knickknacks of every description - china, glass, rubber plants, aspidistras, statues of the Venus de Milo, Madonnas, family photos, scent bottles and lace mats. There was no bedding as the young man said his parents would not be home till 10 and it was evidently their room. So we said we would go and try and find some supper. He seemed a bit dubious as there was nothing in the neighbourhood. Still, we managed to get a tram to take us to the centre of the town near the Grand Hotel, and we eventually found a restaurant and were taken in charge by an affable waiter who seemed to think we were French. He showed us to a table in a corner, seated us with a flourish, and placed a small French flag on the table. I was terrified that the band would then strike up the Marseillaise, but fortunately not. As the menu was incomprehensible and in Cyrillic characters anyway he took charge and brought us some delicious cutlets well arranged with sort of roses made of mashed potato with chips as petals, very nice. With wine and an orange the dinner cost us £4 but was worth it. We managed to find our way on foot back to the apartment, as the trams were not running. Oh I forgot, the crowd in the restaurant were all singing at the tops of their voices, led by a powerful female who we couldn't see as the band was round the corner. They all seemed very jolly and prosperous looking. Around midnight it seemed that everyone was turned out as it was closing time. We understood it was some sort of holiday or festival next day and they were celebrating. When we got back our hosts were awaiting us, speaking French, and we turned in. Huge gold satin quilts encased in sheet envelopes were on the bed and actually we slept quite well. Tom got up early and nipped into the bathroom but I was held up for ages as there seemed to be various sons of the house who took an age shaving. Tom

On the Hippy Trail

went off to fetch the car, and we left. No one offered us any breakfast so we stopped at a corner bakery for doughnuts and what we thought was coffee in glass mugs, but it turned out to be ice cold, very thick and tasting like nothing on earth. I think some kind of grain was involved as it seemed popular and doubtless nourishing but not very cheering on a cold morning.

Saturday 6th. The drive through Bulgaria was quite interesting and roads not bad. Met a couple of bearded young men leading a laden camel, probably Germans. Had the usual long wait at the Turkish customs and were told to report to the Istanbul customs within 48 hours. This meant staying 2 nights instead of one. Very monotonous dull drive to Istanbul though Edirne looked interesting and typically Eastern. Suddenly the people seemed colourful and there were dogs and cats which we didn't see anywhere else. It was quite nice to be back again.

Stayed Saturday at the Cinar Hotel at Yesilkoy, very nice. Next night at Bebek Hotel, with a super room overlooking the Bosporus. Had dinner at a fish restaurant where we were properly "had" as we were given a lobster as hors d'oevres and then found it cost 70 lira.

Monday 8th. Went to the customs. Told we should have gone straight to Ankara as the Vauxhall had been registered there. Now we should have to leave the car in Istanbul while they wrote to Ankara for instructions. Or we could drive on, report to Ankara, and pay a fine. When we got to Ankara, Tom was told that he would have to leave the car with the customs in Ankara till he got a residence permit, or pay 200 lira and a fine as well. You can't win. The residents permit will take at least 3 weeks. Meanwhile the embassy say not to go near the customs.

Anyway we had a glorious drive to Ankara, sunny and not cold. Had lunch at a roadside park by a lake, and it was marvellous. Arrived about 5.30 driving straight into the smog again. Found the flat in good order, but no electricity. Greeted with cries of joy by our neighbour Mrs Yardimci and asked in. First we unloaded the car and borrowed some matches. Then we went over to the Yardimcis. When the doctor came home, now a senator of course, he rang up a pal in the electricity department who sent up a man within half an hour to reconnect us. Very efficient. They kindly asked us to pot luck - kofte and macaroni and stewed apples, and we had a pleasant evening with them, slightly hard work though having to talk French to him and English to her. By the time we got back the electricity was on and we could see what we were doing and do some unpacking. A thick film of grime and dust over everything, but otherwise all seemed well and no burglars.

Eyeball to Eyeball

Our journey from door to door was 2,680 and we should have taken about a week. Our longest drive was 375 miles. Couldn't do vast distances because of the fog and the early darkness. There was very little traffic all the way, and all of it driving well, until we got to Turkey, where the manners are shocking particularly at night with headlights being turned full on as they get up to one, cutting in and generally behaving in a thoroughly selfish manner. Only saw about 4 crashes on the Istanbul road, mostly lorries. One had been full of apples and they were all over the road, on the Boludag, with the driver standing by with a bandage over one eye haranging a friend evidently saying it wasn't his fault by the gestures.

I lay on my bed. It was our second day in Ankara. I thought to myself - How shall I ever stick two years here. We did not know a soul, no one knew us, we didn't know much about the country and it all seemed alien and unfamiliar. The afternoon sun streamed in through the sketchily curtained windows and there seemed to be not a breath of air. There was a peculiar slightly unpleasant smell everpresent, which we traced to our bathroom, and more particularly to the foam rubber bathmat which proved to be saturated with musty smelling water. By shutting the door firmly between the rooms we could forget about it, but it hit one in the face after one had been out and had come in again. We found later by experience that most Turkish hotel bathrooms smelt, but not often of bathmat. Mostly the plumbing was faulty, even in brand new hotels. Water would shoot out of the most unlikely places, mostly all over the floor, but seldom where it was intended to flow.

We had driven out from England in early October. I wasn't particularly keen to leave England again, as we had only just moved into the first house we had ever owned in Cornwall, and had furnished it and made it homely for the summer holidays. Then this offer of a job in Turkey had arrived, and we didn't think that we could afford to turn it down. After all it was for only two years - we could moss up a little capital maybe to replace that which had gone on the house. Also, and not least, was the ever-present school bills looming up, which on a pension were not funny. Anyway, the pros and cons were weighed, and we found ourselves on the way, and I was to come back by train in a couple of months, to have Christmas at home with the children and to arrange for the letting of the house, as it was all too much of a rush at the beginning.

We had left England on 28th September - a fateful day with us. On that day Tom had originally left England for Kenya in 1936 to join the Colonial Administrative Service. And on the same day twenty five years later we left Kenya again on retirement. Our daughter Jocelyn's birthday was on that day too. And here we were again, setting forth into the unknown again on that same

On the Hippy Trail

date. It was now Jocelyn's twenty first birthday, and so as a treat (we hoped) she was coming with us as far as Cologne, have the weekend there, and fly back to London again. She had had some odd birthdays in the past. Perhaps the most bizarre was the one spent in Kabul Afghanistan. We had been invited that evening to a party given by a couple of Russians who were working for the United Nations, as we were. They were a delightful couple. One, Yirmikoff, was the Expert in Building and Architecture, and the other Goutoff was his interpreter, who in fact was quite as highly qualified as Yirmikoff. The Russians were usually sent in pairs on these assignments, and they always lived together and usually went to every function together. Perhaps it was handy for the UN as they got two experts for the price of one. Anyway the party was a riot, with every nationality represented and vodka flowing freely, accompanied by a kind of rolled up pickled herring. Somehow it got known that it was Jocelyn's birthday, and then she had an awful time being toasted in turn by everyone, and much too shy to reciprocate. Vodka is supposed to be downed at one gulp which made it even more embarrassing.

Anyway it is time we had a celebration in a nice hotel half way down the Rhine. We were staying in Cologne, and had done a day trip. Unfortunately the weather was horrid, grey and cloudy and my recollections of the scene are uniformly drab and chilly. Next day we found our way with some difficulty to the Airport, which was surprisingly small and modest for such a large city we thought, and saw her winging her way back to London again.

AIRING THE TENTS March 15th 1966

The Goldsmiths rang us up a few days ago to ask whether we would like to join them in a camping weekend "to shake the cobwebs out of the tents". So we said yes. Tom hasn't got much to do anyway so decided to take Saturday off.

On Wednesday we had supper with them and decided what to do about food etc. I was to do Saturday lunch and Sunday breakfast, and Bridget would do supper on Saturday and lunch on Sunday, and we both brought a few spares. My contribution was a tin full of rock cakes and some oranges which were very popular, also some salad.

The rendezvous was 7.30 on Saturday morning and we were only 5 minutes late. The worst part of these trips is the loading up and carting down stuff to the car and it always takes longer than you think. Also trying to leave the flat tidy to come back to and everything turned off. In actual fact we left a light in the kitchen on, and on our return thought that burglars must have got in.

Eyeball to Eyeball

After filling up with petrol we managed to get away about 7.50, the Goldsmiths in front. We stopped at Polatli (40 miles away) at a mobil station to get the tyres checked, and found that one was no less than 30, and the others about 25, the recommended pressure for our Michelin X tyres being 18 and 22. So that made a great difference. The clot at the garage hadn't a clue how to test the tyres but luckily (!) we had a tyre pressure gauge.

Past Eskisehir, which we reached about 10.30, we made a steady 60 to 70 mph. Then to Kutahya (about 11.45) where we hope to go over a pottery, but were told that they shut from 12 to 1. So we decided to have our picnic lunch and return later. We went a little way up an atrocious track which appeared to lead to the citadel, but were soon stopped by a narrow Roman? gateway and there the road petered out. So we parked perilously and ate our lunch (quiche lorraine and salad) perched on some rocks above the road, with crowds of children milling round below. At 1 we found our way with some difficulty to the pottery. We never discovered how many there were in the town but probably several. They agreed to show us over it and we saw more or less the whole process except for the glazing. The most interesting was the painting by a lot of young girls after the pots had been fired. They rubbed transfers of the broad outlines on to the plain pots, and then outlined the pattern in brown pigment (which turned black when fired again) and also filled in the design freehand with leaves and flowers. They used a brush made of a goose quill for a handle and a piece of donkey mane specially shaped for the "brush". Later the colours were added, all looking quite different from the final product. We bought a few things but obviously the best things went to Ankara or Istanbul and prices were higher too.

By this time it was about 2 so we decided to hit the trail. Our objective were some Greek and Roman ruins about 60 kms on and the Goldsmiths were told that you could camp under the temple, with trees all round and a river. However, when we reached the village of Cavdarhisar and turned right, crossed an old Roman bridge, and found ourselves under the temple, a splendid sight, with lots of tall pillars (restored but very well done) and a huge sort of crypt underneath. One surprising thing was a huge carving of the goddess Cybele on a stone, set up below the temple of Zeus, and it had not been touched, no stones had been thrown at it and the features were absolutely intact. Some custodians arrived and said we could camp right there or move on, but we thought it would be a bit too public and right in the village so that we should never get any privacy at all. So after exploring a bit we decided to get on and look for a site. After about 5 miles we passed through another village and found a pleasant site. To get to it we had to drive along a small river bed with water flowing, but fortunately the bottom was hard, and then up a bank on to a grassy flat place

On the Hippy Trail

surrounded by poplar trees. John tried to cross this sward as he thought it looked more sheltered on the other side, but it was very wet and muddy and he stuck fast. We pulled him out with our car and some rope and then decided to stay on the side which did not seem to be under water. It was getting quite chilly with a strong wind blowing, so we parked the cars together to get a bit of shelter and put up the tents. The Goldsmiths was one you inflate and went up in a few minutes. Ours was the small one so didn't take long either. We set up the chairs and tables and cooking stoves behind the tents, and by that time it was Martini time. Although Bridget and I were off drink for lent we decided to have a dispensation chiefly for medicinal reasons, as we had to get warm somehow. She then warmed up the supper and Phillippa had hers before going to bed. The full moon got up and we sat by its light, not wanting to waste the batteries of our lights. Various groups of men went past and then back again evidently wanting to have a good look at the mad foreigners. Then some of the bolder ones crossed the river and came up to say hos geldiniz and shake us all by the hand. They usually told us there was a hotel in the village and why didn't we come and spend the night there instead of out in the cold, and to each group John Goldsmith would give a flowery and garbled explanation that we were tired of Ankara and houses and all we wanted was the sky and stars and fresh air. They obviously thought we were stark staring mad (and they were not so far wrong either). We must have had at least 60 visitors, mostly in large groups, which included the elders of the village and the nahir, then various younger chaps ending up with a lot of teenagers. Most of them accepted our English cigarettes though they didn't all smoke them there and then. Some brought us some firewood for the fire that, with some difficulty, we had got going. The last lot got very chatty and topics ranged from the weather to football (Liverpool United and Manchester were specially mentioned) to Churchill (now with God) to Ataturk (also with God), how there was one God for everyone etc. etc. At last they all went and by that time it was 10 o'clock. We turned in after a final night-cap in all our clothes (in my case tights, warm vest, shirt, polo-neck thick sweater over another sweater, dressing gown over all, and my hot water bottle. Inside a sleeping bag with blanket over all. Tom had our very uncomfortable camp bed. At once I heard deafening snores from next door so was glad to think that the Goldsmiths were having a good night. They thought the same of us, but we later discovered it was the dog which (as usual) had adopted us, and slept on the ground outside the tent. He must have been perishing as by morning the ground was covered by a hard frost, and we had all been shivering most of the night. Somehow we survived and by the time we crawled out in the dawn the sun was beginning to peep over the hill in front and we got up our circulations. The men and Phillippa got warmed up by climbing the hill to take some photographs, Bridget and I by cooking eggs and bacon and coffee. A few

Eyeball to Eyeball

visitors came along but were rather shyer in daylight and a few small boys were smartly sent on their way as we didn't care for spectators of everything we did.

After a leisurely breakfast we started to dismantle the camp and pack up which didn't take very long. To get in and out of the site we had to get the cars between two trees, a very narrow space with only fractions of an inch to spare. Going out was a bit tricky as we had to get through a very muddy patch first in which we both skidded somewhat. Then down into the stream and away. We went back to the ruins and the village of Cavdarhisar and took some photographs and got warm in the sun. Then we walked over some ploughed fields to the theatre and stadium which were in a very ruinous state through some earthquakes in olden days. By this time it was about 12 noon, and so we had to think about getting away so as not to be too late, so reluctantly we tore ourselves away, first stopping to take some photographs of the bridge and some women in baggy mauve satin trousers washing clothes in the river. We had lunch at the top of a hill in a grove of coniferous bushes with skirts down to the ground like whirling dervishes. We set up the table and chairs and basked in the sun till about 1.30. Then reluctantly piled into our respective cars and headed back to Ankara.

The name of the ancient ruins we had visited was Aesani.

THE HAWKERS OF ANKARA

Life in Ankara is made more interesting by the hawkers who have practically disappeared in Britain (with the possible exception of ice cream vendors). From sunrise to sunset they are on their way, and apparently scores doing the same trade. At intervals during the day come the boys selling rings of bread with sesame seeds stuck on the outside. These are carried on a tray balanced on the head, sometimes in a glass walled box but more often not. They look extremely tempting, these "semits" but having on a number of occasions seen the tray go flying and the semits all over the ground, and then the loving way they are piled up symmetrically all over again with a grimy hand, the temptation to buy is not so great. But they are very popular with office and shop workers who do not have much or any breakfast, and with children who ware them on their arms like bracelets until they are hungry. They are sold at street corners and station platforms and fresh batches straight from the bakery are taken round the residential areas every few hours.

Another ubiquitous hawker is the eskici - the rag-and-bone man. His chief trade is in bottles and newspaper. The airmail editions of the English newspapers are highly prized being extremely suitable for the rolling of home-made cigarettes, and one gets about 5 lira or 4/- a kilo for these. The eskici will buy anything at

On the Hippy Trail

all and as he goes past with his mournful cry of "es-ki" he keeps a weather eye on all the windows of the buildings on his way for the slightest sign of encouragement, and then in a trice he is outside your front door asking if you have anything to sell. When foreigners come to the end of their tours the news seems to go round by bush telegraph and they are besieged by eskicis willing to buy old and worn out clothes and household goods old and new. If there is some superior article to be sold such as a fridge or cooker or wireless, or furniture, he brings a rather superior sort of person clad in suits and tie, who evidently keeps a second hand shop, and very good prices are given, though a certain amount of bargaining takes place before all are mutually satisfied.

Another familiar visitor is the boyaci, or shoe-shine boy, who is a great boon to those not very keen on cleaning their own shoes. He goes round the residential areas shouting his particular slogan - "boy-a-ci" and something which sounds like "irradio" and if you call out of your window up he comes to sit on your landing and shine all the shoes in the house at about 5d each pair. Sometimes he will sit down stairs surrounded by dozens of shoes collected from the whole block of flats, and in due course he will appear with the right pairs, all immaculately polished. Of course it is lazy not to clean ones own shoes, but who is one to deprive a man of his livelihood? There are boyacis who have beats all over the town, sometimes in rows of shiny brass stands all decorated with brightly coloured pictures of lakes and mountains and pin up girls in provocative poses, with the brass covers to the pots of polish all twinkling in the sun. When a likely looking customer approaches, they start drumming with their brushes on their boxes as a hint to the customer, and very often he will stop and have his shoes shined while standing on the pavement. The boyacis are most meticulous in putting pieces of cardboard down each shoe so the socks will not get smeared.

Every now and then a basket seller will come round, with piles of laundry baskets and other types, though we found the most difficult thing to get was an ordinary waste paper basket. There were plenty in brightly coloured plastic, but one had to search for a long time before finding an ordinary wicker one. Then there is the seller of brooms and brushes, mostly the kind like a bunch of reeds tied at one end, which is the most common form of broom in Turkey and comes in various sizes, and is surprisingly effective for sweeping dust into corners but not much good when you are trying to get it into a dustpan.

All through the winter, and even into mid summer one sees an old man shrouded in furs. He will have a large moth-eaten bear skin (brown) over one arm and another over his shoulder and in his hands a bunch of fox or stone marten furs. They are cured in a way, but would require some further treatment one would

Eyeball to Eyeball

think. I once saw the poor man having a tug of war with a large dog who had one end of his bear skin in its teeth and was determined not to let go till it had killed it.

Everyday, at the same time, a yamurtaci or egg man will come round, and he had the most rousing voice of all. He pushes an ancient pram covered in blue oilcloth (this is a must for all egg men), the pattern of blue checks is invariable, some have a bicycle attached to the pram, but only a few can afford that. He also sells yoghurt in large aluminium pans. The eggs are very fresh and are even stamped with the date and I have only once or twice had a bad one, which was always replaced next day. In the spring and summer there are always people passing selling tomatoes and apples and oranges or strawberries (the season for strawberries lasts from April to July). They are weighted on an unreliable contraption held by the top in one hand and with pans on either side and are supposed to be accurate though they don't look it. Prices are usually fixed and only rarely will they be brought down by bargaining.

My favourite hawker is the balloon man who frequently passes shouting "Balloon, balloon, balloon" and he holds a huge bunch on the end of a string. Sometimes the string is let out to its fullest extent and you see the bunch of balloons floating along at roof-top level several storeys high. One seldom sees them selling a balloon, but they do cheer one up just to look at them.

In Istanbul and other towns there are the drink sellers, and they have polished brass containers slung over their shoulders, with all sorts of bells and dingle dangles hanging from the pointed conical top, and the glasses are kept in a bandolier round the waist. What the drinks are I do not know, but there is something which looks rather like cold tea with a slight head on it and tastes bitter, but is evidently very popular and refreshing.

THE MEDITERRANEAN

Started off from Ankara about 6 a.m. Filled up at TP station on the outskirts, tyres tested etc. and off we went. Good road through Polatli to Cay, where we turned off via the short cut to Egridir. Most of it quite good "yellow" road, only the last bit over the mountains could be tricky in wet weather. We came down the other side to find ourselves at the head of the lake, where there was an enormous swamp simply crammed with birds of all descriptions. We had a picnic lunch and then went on to the hotel. This is new this year and was started by a man who had a motor spares shop in Istanbul. He greeted us warmly, clad only in yellow bathing trunks and we were given the pick of all the rooms as there didn't seem to be many people there. We then proceeded to the lake shore where we had a lovely bathe, only marred by the attentions of a particularly virulent type of fly which bit Tom and me continuously, but not, for some reason Jos. Back to the hotel about 5 and T. went out to paint a picture. When it got dark we sat outside and the only lights were some neon ones on the terrace facing outwards. No lights were put on in the hotel except for the kitchen because of the dudus. We had dinner in almost complete darkness too so one really did not know what one was eating.

Friday 5th. Marcus's birthday. Breakfast at Isparta, a very good breakfast too, though the lokanta was the filthiest I have ever seen, the floors having never been washed since the day it was built I should think. The proprietor had a mania for calendars and there were 9 at least all round the walls. So far so good. The road out of Isparta is being rebuilt and conditions were chaotic and very few warning notices about the various hazards, with clouds of volcanic dust over everything. After Dinar we found the road closed altogether, and we had to take a diversion which was quite good. Past Acigol where we saw lots of flamingoes. After that the road was tarmac all the way to the coast. It got hotter and hotter as we descended, then took a side road to Aphrodisias. Pictured it on the top of a nice cool mountain but not a bit of it. The road rose very gradually, nasty cobbles and ruts most of the way. Had a hot lunch on the road beyond the ruins, then we turned back to explore them. I was a bit disappointed. Excavations had been going on and one had to guess what all the ruins were, and we were pursued by a crowd of giggling girls who kept peeping at us round every corner we came to. So on we went to Kusadasi where we set up camp at the BP mocamp. Had a glorious bathe and supper in the cafeteria place which had a cool breeze. T. and I had a rented tent for one night as we were rather tired and Jos slept in the open.

Saturday August 6. Spent the morning lazing on the beach and trying to sunbathe painlessly. After lunch we were just having a siesta when a large American car drove up and asked us to move as we were occupying their site. Actually there was a derelict hut there and we used it to tie an awning to, thinking that it was never used. The owner was Mr McGregor from Soke where he runs a liqorice factory and they come here every weekend. So we cleared up and left our stuff behind the hut and went off to see Priene, thinking it wasn't very far. It was not far in mileage but a very slow twisty road, and from Soke onwards an appalling track. As there were no sign posts we kept asking villagers where Priene was and none of them had heard of it. However we at last found the road and inadequate parking space. It was a most impressive city with a commanding position over the plain which was once the sea. It is laid out very well with roads in straight lines, a good little theatre and senate house, and even the fish and meat market still there, and the dwelling houses all in rows with

Eyeball to Eyeball

drainage etc. By the time we got back to Kusadasi it was 7.30 and we stopped for dinner at a fish restaurant where we sat on a terrace a few feet above the sea. Back to camp where we found the McGregors had left the hut open for us, so Jos slept in it and T. and I outside.

Sunday August 7. We couldn't go till 7 as the office did not open till then so we had breakfast and a bathe before that. The road was quite good as far as Milas, though forestsand beside the beautiful lake Bafa with ruins on its islands. At Milas we turned off to a pretty bad road to Bodrum which we reached about 11. We went round the castle first and it was just as well we did as they firmly closed it at 12 and turfed everyone out. The castle was really splendid and unobtrusively restored. Right on the edge of the sea it had been rebuilt by the Crusaders in 15 something incorporating many stones from the Mauseleum, one of the wonders of the world. Somebody had bombed it at some time but we couldn't quite make out who. There was a French tower and an Italian tower and an English one. By the time 12 came we were feeling pretty hot and tired so looked for a beach. Found one quite near, but not very appealing as it seemed to have been the town rubbish dump, covered with bits of paper, rags, bandages, melon rinds etc. However we got as far along as we could and the water was clean anyway. Had lunch at a cesme a little way out of Bodrum in the pine forests and could wash all the sticky karpuz juice off straight away.

We then made for Marmaris, going back almost to Milas and then back on to the main road again, through Yatagan where we had some tea, paid for by a young man who came and sat with us and tried out his not-very-good English. Through Mugla where we turned off to Marmaris. A fantastic road down an escarpment of 1500 feet just like the Rift Valley. Met all sorts of buses and dolmuses coming home from a day at the sea. Most of them were grossly overloaded with passengers sitting on the roof as well as squashed inside, singing away at the tops of their voices. We passed a policeman who stopped a dolmus and was looking at its licences etc, and later met a crowd of weary young men who had evidently been turfed off for overcrowding. Another car stopped us and asked us if we had seen the Traffik and where they were. We got to Marmaris as it was getting dark. The only hotel name I knew was the Otel Lydia where various people we knew had stayed, but I was not prepared for such an enormous posh place. There was only one double room left in quite the worst position in the hotel behind the dinning rooms with no view, and they put a third bed in the middle, but we had no alternative but to take it as we couldn't face the thought of turning out again driving 10 kms to Marmaris and looking for an iki bucuk in the dark. We had a pretty stifling night, mitigated by cold showers at intervals. Quite a nice dinner on the terrace, but as at all big hotels the helpings were a bit meagre and on the whole unintresting.

On the Hippy Trail

Monday August 8th. Had a glorious bathe before breakfast. The Otel Lydia is in a superb position right on the sea and surrounded by mountains enclosing the Gulf of Marmaris. We went into the town and walked about a bit pursued by various touts who wanted to show us the sights. Otherwise it was a rather charming little place with sponge fishing caiques in the harbour. Did some shopping - and went back the way we had come up the escarpment, with not so much traffic this time. Turned off before we got to Mugla, along a good gravel road to Koycegis. Here was an inland lake with a small opening to the sea. It looked very green and inviting so we stopped on the "front" and had a bathe, not particularly pleasant as the water was so warm and opaque and muddy, and there were too many young men and boys hovering around watching everything we did. We had our lunch in a bahce which was cool and breezy.

Can't remember what the next bit of road was like but it wasn't too bad, a bit twisty and dusty I think. About 10 miles before we came to Fethiye we spied a delightful looking cove down below with quite a good track leading to it so thought we would have a bathe. Found a gorgeous little bay with a few tents dotted about belonging to some German, French and English tourists, and were able to set up our tent in the key position on the edge of the sea, with a hefty wooden table and benches beside us, in fact two, which made a lot of difference. There were not very many mosquitoes and we had a scratch supper before it got really dark and went to bed early. Next morning a bathe before breakfast and we decided to spend another day here as it was so perfect.

Tuesday 9th. Went into Fethiye to collect some food and look around. Climbed to the rock tombs carved in the cliffs above the town, most impressive and luckily in deep shade at that hour of day. Fethiye itself is not very attractive and we were glad we weren't staying there. The gulf looks very shallow and enclosed and it was very hot and humid. We bought some groceries and fruit and torch batteries and returned with all speed to Camlikoy, our bay, and plunged into the sea again. T. painted in the afternoon, J and I lazed. Had midnight(?) bathe and enjoyed the phosphorescence.

Wednesday 10th. Reluctantly we left Camlikoy, we couldn't have found a more perfect spot anywhere and the temperature was just right. Filled up with petrol and some fruit, and hit the trail once more, over the mountains first through rolling parkland before climbing. Lovely road from the scenery point of view and very little traffic. We suddenly came to the top of a pass and found ourselves in a classical ruined city with a theatre very well preserved, and sarcophagi on tall pillars all round it. It was Xanthos, and a guide roared up on a motor bike to show us round. We saw what we could but didn't want to go too far as it was

Eyeball to Eyeball

beginning to warm up (8 o'clock) and we didn't know what awaited us further on. Some 50 miles on we came to Kas after a lovely drive along the edge of the sea, sometimes down by the waters edge at other times right up above. The sea was an incredible blue (Mediterranean) and the rocks were reddish yellow. We stopped at a little bay and had a wonderful swim, and T. found the remnants of what was evidently an amphora. We collected all the pieces we could and put them in a string bag, with a view to piecing it together again during the long winter evenings (what a hope). Kas was not quite what I had expected. It was a sleepy little place with an indescribable air of lethargy about it. Everyone looked poor and downtrodden and we couldn't get a cold drink anywhere. Bought some tomatoes and fruit and I proceeded to leave the kikapu containing them behind, but it was not worth going back for. We saw the promontory we thought the Warrs were buying in an extremely inaccessible place except by boat. The next bit of road to Finike was not bad, narrow and winding but again next to no traffic. We had no horn by that time so it was just as well we didn't meet anything. Finike was much nicer than I had expected, had quite a lively air. We drove along a long stretch of sandy beach which was also the runway for small aeroplanes and thought of camping in the dunes, but thought we might be pestered by people, so decided to stay in an hotel. First we washed the car thoroughly in a fresh water stream where various other people were doing the same. There was a small aircraft next door which had been spraying crops recently, judging from the smell of flit which emanated from it. As we were cruising along slowly trying to find the two no-star hotels which were in the book we were beckoned to by a young man who took us to the Touristic Otel Kosk, which proved to be very nice. Very nice rooms with view of the sea and big verandahs on which we sat in the evening. I had thought it was ideal from the point of view of a bathe before breakfast, but changed my mind when I saw the black oily waves trickling up the beach, though some soldiers were swimming there. Had a first class dinner in the restoran on the roof of the hotel. Didn't sleep much because of the extreme heat and stuffiness and had to keep on getting up and having cold showers.

Thursday 11th. Up early and away before 6.30. Here we left the sea and went across the Bey Daglari mountains. Very beautiful it was with tall pines and some delightful streams and waterfalls. Had breakfast by the side of the road before the sun reached us. We got on to a kind of plateau at Elmali where it was treeless and brown and nothing but huge herds of black goats streaming along like toy soldiers in lines. Korkuteli was not like my idea of it. Quite a big place with lots of shops and mosques. Bought two shukas and some sardines.

On down the other side, through pine forests until we came to Antalya about 1. Drove to our old camping place at the far end of the beach. But it was not nearly so nice, masses of paper and muck everywhere. We spent the afternoon there under our same trees, and about 5 went into Antalya to get a few things and look around. It is still incredibly beautiful in its position and the mountains, though they were not as clear as in the spring. By this time I was feeling rather ill and realised I had a return of cystitis, probably through sitting about in wet bathing dresses or clothes. I got some pills from the chemist which seemed to be for my complaint. I sat in the car while T. and J. went round the harbour. Had dinner on the roof of the Ankara Lokantasi. At about 8.30 we thought we had better go and establish ourselves for the night at a place on the beach where there was a notice saying Aile Kampi Yeri. We drove in at the gates with a flourish only to find ourselves axle deep in loose shingle and unable to move in any direction. Some people drifted up and told us that we should have parked out on the bit beside the road, but that was so helpful. There was absolutely nothing to say so and no gate to prevent us driving in. We tried to get out, and a few ineffectual attempts were made to lift us up, but it was obviously no good and so we unpacked everything off the car and set up our camp by the gate. I have never felt so much of a refugee. However we had a very good night in spite of everything because there were no mosquitoes and it was delightfully cool.

Friday 12th. We were up needless to say at first light, and had breakfast. One or two people appeared and muttered something about a jeep arriving at 7. So we waited and waited till 7 and nothing happened so T. began digging in earnest. A few people helped but the majority just looked on as if it was none of their business. Maybe it was because of T.'s uncomplimentary remarks the night before. Or else they were business men and didn't want to mess up their office clothes. Anyway someone brought a couple of boards, covered in nails which had to be removed much to their surprise. Gradually with the aid of the jack and the boards under the wheels and a lot of digging with our invaluable spade T. got the car out. A bathe was then imperative, though I was not supposed to swim because of my complaint, and anyway didn't really want to.

In to Antalya for a look round and then a cool drink on the terrace of the teachers club. We were a bit later going off than we had planned, but not so bad considering.

First stop was Aspendos as J. hadn't seen it. I sat around and they went up to the top. A lot of work has been done since we were last here. Then on to Side, where again I sat while they explored. Then we went on to rather a nice beach where they swam. Had lunch at the top of the cliff rather nice. Saw that shark Suat Bey sitting having lunch on the terrace of his new hotel, the Pamphilia.

Eyeball to Eyeball

Passed the BP Mocamp at Alanya so-called, in reality about 40 kms away, but didn't like it much as a site, very little shade and miles away, not much of a beach either. On to Incekum where we found a nice position, though it did not look quite so nice as it had when we camped there two years before. It probably always looks better in the spring. Anyway we established our camp, they had a bathe, and later we went in to Alanya. Walked around a bit on the harbour and then had dinner in a lokanta on the sand. Had to move our chairs when the sea swished in over our feet. Masses of pointer-type dogs around. Back to Incekum and a good night.

Saturday 13th. The last lap almost of our journey. The road to Gzipasi was good tarmac. Then the road was not bad gravel, which suddenly deteriorated considerably, and we found ourselves confronted with a large gap in the road of about 200 yards or more. There was simply no road there. Some road people told us we would have to wait 3 hours till the road was made. So we sat and watched three bulldozers and a tractor thing with a hook making the road, and I must say they did it remarkably. At the other side of the gap was a line of traffic headed by a 2 cheveaux (?) and an English party in a Land Rover. Behind us were a couple of buses and quite a few cars, Germans, British, French, Italian and two Turkish taxis. The buses were full of villagers returning to Mersin and one of the girls talked English quite well. Everyone strolled about to while away the time and chatted. Eventually we saw the work was finished though the road looked like a ploughed field with sundry large rocks which had not been cleared away. On the right was a 800 feet drop to the sea, so the road was just a narrow ledge. The other people came over first, then it was our turn. We had the same sort of conditions for the next 10 miles and had to wait several times while mechanical shovels bit into the cliffs. At one spot a wretched little Volkswagon containing a German couple - he in a beard and she in a bikini, whizzed past us so as to be in front. Then the two Turkish taxis came along blowing their horns loudly and continuously and squeaked past though I tried to stop them by holding the doors open. Though I would rather, personally, that they were in front of us rather than behind. At last we came down on to the plains again by the sea and took a turning which said Annemoria. This turned out to be a ruined Roman city of quite considerable size. Had lunch and the others a bathe, and various other of the cars which had been behind us at the road block turned up too, the two Italians and an Austrian family. On to Annemur, which was quite a magnificent building or had been in its better days. Now it is just a shell and a large bit in the middle where you park your car. There were not many people.

Last stage on to Silifke and Korikos. Tarmac road very good all the way from now on. Got to the Mocamp about 6. Set up the tent, more for privacy when

On the Hippy Trail

dressing than anything else - I only set foot in it once. Dinner in the restaurant. We slept out, and have never had so many mosquitos. They were terrible, bit through sheets and shukas and we didn't get much sleep.

Sunday 14th. Last day alas. Got away by 8. Bathed in the shingle bay where we had seen tanks landing in the spring. Gave Alahan a miss as it was really too hot for intense climbing. We did stop at the place described by Nancy Downes, and found some fossilled shells which was rather a thrill, helped by three small children, Meryam, ? and Mustapha who wore a girls dress down to his ankles. They knew what we were looking for and showed us where some of the fossils were, and kept handing us minute shells which they had dug out. We gave them some sweets and they seemed pleased. Lunch just after the top of the pass, under a shady tree. Uneventful journey home, and found that Marcus had returned, complete with 5 friends to stay the night. It was nice to get the car unpacked so rapidly, and then T. had to go out and forage for some food and drink as there was to be a celebration party in the evening. We went to bed and left them to it. The scrambled eggs and sausages seemed to be much appreciated anyway.

Seljuk Citadel near Ephesus

CHAPTER 18

Memories of Turkey

BY MICHAEL

After being offered a place at Peterhouse, Cambridge in January 1963, it was decided that there was no need to stay on at Pangbourne to do further A levels in the summer. So I left school soon afterwards to start a "gap" in Turkey before going to Cambridge in the autumn. Jos, Marcus and I had just spent Christmas with Mum in Storrington, Sussex, and since Mum was due to fly out to Turkey in January, it was convenient for me to go with her. So she and I flew out together, spending a night in Athens en route for Ankara, where we were able to visit the Acropolis, and see a bit of Athens.

Ankara was a new city, established only in the 1920's as the capital of the country. But it was increasing rapidly in size due to the continual influx of people from the rural areas of Anatolia. We had a nice flat in Cankaya, up a hill with a wonderful view over the city. In winter it tended to be covered by smog, but this was a relatively minor irritant compared with the many positive factors about the city.

After I arrived we discussed when it would be best to start at Cambridge, as October seemed a bit too soon. I felt I needed more time to find my feet, and mature a bit. We thus thought it would be a good idea to start off with a few months in Turkey, and then spend some time in France and gain a better knowledge of French. So I wrote to Peterhouse suggesting that I delay going up until October 1965, and its reply was positive. So I made steps to study in France, and eventually chose to go to the University of Grenoble.

In the meantime, I needed to get dug into some useful and interesting activities, and to feel that I was using that "free" time to good effect. There were a number of possibilities. I had wanted to get some sort of formal job, but this proved elusive and I so I ended up doing a number of things which looking back, contributed to my education, and helped to make the gap worthwhile. The time enabled me to start to learn Turkish, be exposed to teaching English to foreigners, to learn to type, to do a lot of reading, sketching and painting, to

Eyeball to Eyeball

travel around parts of Turkey, and to get to know many interesting and wonderful people.

I started off by joining Mum at the Turkish-American Center, learning Turkish with a number of expatriate ladies. This was a lot of fun, and I studied quite hard at home to get a good grounding in the language, which was then consolidated when I went traveling. I enjoyed this, as well as trying to practice it with Turks I met in shops, taxis, buses etc. The mere fact of saying something in another language is half way to learning it.

Over time, I was able to meet a few people who wanted to improve their English. There was Ardar, a medical doctor in training whom I enjoyed visiting and talking to, and another high school student who was my first paid student. I could have done with a bit of formal training, but this was to come later.

Mum had a wonderful idea that I should learn to type. My hand-writing was never the greatest, and so she gave me the same Pitman's type-writing manual which she had used back in the late 1930's, and set me to work on her ancient type-writer. It took me a month to learn the keyboard and to type at a reasonable speed, and from then onwards, it was a question of practice and increasing the speed This very practical skill proved to be one of the most valuable ones I ever learned. Later I typed all my papers at Cambridge, a fairly rare event in those days and at work, I typed a lot of my drafts. Subsequently, I became a dab hand at the computer, and this increased my productivity many-fold. I was thereafter never separated from a variety of typewriters, from a portable Olivetti Lettera, to an electric Olivetti, and leading up to a series of Toshiba lap top computers. These enabled me both to present decent work, but also as Mum always found, to let my thoughts flow more clearly.

To fill in some of the time, I enjoyed using the British Council library and doing some reading on subjects which my earlier school routine did not provide time for. I remember reading up about Ataturk, the founder of Modern Turkey, and the incredible changes he had managed to bring about in that country. I also read a number of biographies, including of the sculptor Jacob Epstein, which was a real eye opener to the world of sculpture, and the controversies he created. I studied a few art books, and tried to do some sketching and painting and learn from Pa's experience. This was complemented by a lot of drawing and a bit of painting, with the purpose of getting my eye slightly more aesthetically inclined.

On the cultural side, I used to go to play reading evenings with people from the British Embassy. John Goulden was one, a bright young Foreign Office spark,

Memories of Turkey

who had done an intensive course learning Turkish before going to Turkey, and was the one in the Embassy responsible for reading the Turkish newspapers. I would have loved that job. He subsequently became British Ambassador to Turkey. We also went periodically to the theatre. I vividly remember the magnificent rendering in Turkish of the musical "Kiss me Kate" One of the avid theatre-goers was Ismet Inonu, the Prime Minister, who was in his nineties, and rather hard of hearing. It was a reminder of the radical change which Turkish society had gone through since its founder, Kemal Ataturk decreed a modern, secular state, and determined to embrace all things western.

Dad's job as an Adviser in Community Development with the State Planning Organization opened up a number of contacts, some of whom I met informally at dinner parties and social evenings. These were real eye openers, and I was always greatly stimulated to meet such a lot of interesting people. Two of these were rather crucial for my future: Art Duning was a Social Affairs adviser with the UN, teaching at the Social Services Academy in Ankara. His colleague, Dick Scott, was a Fulbright Scholar. There were also Lewis and Mary Anderson, a Canadian couple. He was a family planning adviser from the Population Council. I saw a lot of Art and his wife, Rosemary, and enjoyed many meals with them.

Then there was Don Stadtner, who had been invited by the Dunings to spend six months in Turkey, doing a semester at the American School. in Ankara. I struck up a wonderful friendship with Don. He was a very bright American from Stockton, California, who was adapting to his first visit out of the US, and to a new high school. He had a wonderful sense of humour, and was intrigued to meet his first Brit. During the Easter break from school, we decided to travel to the south coast of Turkey. We took local buses which sped through the day and night, vast distances, and traveled to Mersin. We then hitch-hiked west along the coast and camped at an old Crusader castle near Silifke. Neither of us had hitch-hiked before but it turned out to be one of the most enjoyable trips either of us had ever taken.

It was fun meeting a wide variety of people, mostly Turks, who were also intrigued to meet us. It was here that I could practise my infant Turkish. We did a bit of our own cooking with a gas stove. To round things off, we tasted some of the local liqueurs, particularly the banana one - unforgettable - or cok guzel. One evening, a French couple pitched their tent in the Castle We obviously made rather a lot of noise, and they evacuated. We then continued along the coast to Anamur, where there was another magnificent fort. En route we visited Genet Genehem, or Heaven and Hell, two cavernous holes several

Eyeball to Eyeball

hundred feet deep, apparently created by meteors. Ma and Pa then drove down to Mersin and we returned to Ankara with them.

This first trip was so successful that we decided to go on another one to the Izmir area during the Easter break, which took us to Ephesus, Bergama, Pamukkalle, Aspendos and Istanbul. We had a lot of fun, and plenty of laughs, and it was a most educational trip for both of us.

I also did a bit of traveling with Ma and Pa. Once we went to Antalya, and Konya. Antalya was a beautiful little town, overlooking the bright blue Mediterranean. I remember visiting Perge nearby and its magnificent U-shaped stadium. Dad was always a mine of information about Turkey, gleaned from visits round the country for community development seminars with his Turkish counterparts, and from reading up about the country. I continued to learn from Pa's efforts to share some of the community development experience he had acquired in Kenya and Afghanistan.

Perhaps the most memorable part of my stay in Turkey was my two months in Varto, a small town of about 2,000 people about twenty miles north of Mus (pronounced Moosh), in the eastern part of the country. It was about 500 miles east of Ankara, and 50 miles west of Lake Van. Dick Scott had asked if I would like to join a field trip of fifteen of his students from the Social Services Academy. Their task was to do some research on the impact of modern medicine on traditional values, and health habits. I was placed with two students, and we lived in the local health centre. The other students were scatted in six other villages, all completing the same questionnaires and research project as was being done in Varto.

I decided to do my own study of the village, and tried to write up everything I could about the town, about its people, and about its economy. I walked around the village, mapped it, talked to people, spent time in the tea house, played backgammon, and generally learned a lot of Turkish. I visited the various commercial establishments, including a cheese-making plant, which made vast circular blocks of cheese, measuring two foot in diameter by nine inches thick. I filled a couple of notebooks, but unfortunately never actually typed out a finished study, which of course would have been useful. Dick used to come out every week with his interpreter to check out how things were progressing.

At the end of my two months, I was due to return to Ankara. With no buses that day, I had to hitch-hike to Mus. I had a first short ride which got me out of sight of Varto and while I was waiting by the side of the road for the next ride, I felt the road shake. I looked down at my rucksack. It was wobbling like a jelly. I

Memories of Turkey

myself had to steady myself. It was an earthquake, which lasted about a minute. I didn't think much of it, as earth tremors were quite frequent in those areas. I duly managed to catch a ride, which took me into Mus, where I spent the night prior to catching a bus the next day. By the time I reached Ankara in the evening, I had seen the local newspapers with front page headlines about the earthquake in Varto "Zelzele olmush vartoda". Obviously I had missed a big one, as about 200 people had been killed.

If I had realized at the time, that Varto had been at the epicentre of the earthquake, I might have gone straight back, but I was not to know. When I learned of the full impact of the disaster, I was determined to return. So after a few days at home, I got back on the bus and returned to Mus and then Varto, by which time a British emergency team from Oxfam had arrived from England, and a medical team from Israel, to set up a field hospital. There was not much I could do, except to look round the mud houses which I had known so well, and take stock of the damage. The smell of carnage still persisted in the air, but most of the bodies had been extracted, and the houses had been flattened. The health centre where we had stayed was made of cement blocks and concrete, and had survived intact. The death toll could have been much higher if the earthquake had happened at night, when people were asleep.

Another of my most memorable experiences in Turkey, was getting involved in the Turkish work camp movement. It had been started by an American Quaker, Jim Johnson, who taught at Robert College, an English-speaking University in Istanbul. A number of work camps were organized every year, in which about 20 - 25 young people, foreign and Turkish, participated. Campers paid their way and received free board and lodging.

After Varto, I proceeded to Gaziantep, about a hundred miles east of the Mediterranean, near the Syrian border. I caught a bus from Mus to Gaziantep, passing through Batman and Diyarbakir, the site of one of Turkey's copper mines. This route was way off the beaten track, and currently out of bounds because of the Kurdish problem. I went on a Work Camp in a village near Gaziantep, in the south-west of the country. We helped to build a "hamam" or Turkish bath house in the village. It was a strange project to have chosen, and the locals must have been intrigued to see a bunch of foreigners come into their village and get to work on such a project.

In one month, we could not finish it, but we made a good start. But the main purpose of the exercise was to get people of different nationalities to work together, rather than finish the whole project, which in any case was beyond us, given the time available. We lived in a nearby school house, and ate

Eyeball to Eyeball

communally, and had a lot of enjoyable social evenings, often round the camp fire, at which people's musical and other talents came out. There were a couple of other Brits on this camp, both from Cambridge, who were a lot of fun. A few of the campers were female. They wore western clothes, short shorts and tended to bare rather a lot of leg and flesh. This of course caused a bit of a stir in that traditional moslem village, and one wonders what the villagers really thought about them.

During the weekends, we used to do sight-seeing trips. One weekend, we went to Karkemish, the archaeological site where Lawrence of Arabia worked in the 1920's, just north of the Syrian border. I had never been too interested in archaeology, but the sight of the extensive ruins, dormant for hundreds of year, baking in the harsh Middle Eastern sun and its bright blue skies, made one reflect on past civilizations which were no more, and the forces which made their rise and fall. Other weekends, we went into Gaziantep, where I remember buying some brightly coloured embroidered cloth.

After Gaziantep, I returned to Ankara. I stayed home, while Marcus came out for his holidays from Haileybury. Jos came too, and later started a job looking after the kids of the British Consul in Istanbul. I made a trip to Istanbul, and also with Ma and Pa, to Goreme the famous site of ancient Byzantine churches carved into rock on the Anatolian plateau.

In October, I took a Turkish boat from Istanbul to Marseille, the Ak Deniz (Mediterranean Sea), from where I caugjht a train up to Grenoble to start my French course at the University of Grenoble.

After my first year at Cambridge, I went out to Turkey again in the summer of 1966. I traveled with Marcus, who was still at Haileybury, and Jos on the Orient Express, down through Germany, Yugoslavia and Greece to Istanbul. It was an exciting and quite lengthy trip of three days. Ma and Pa came down to Istanbul to meet us. Pa was in his third and final year in Ankara. They had moved to a lovely large apartment in Kavaklidere, down the hill from our former house in Cankaya. Unfortunately, both Dunings and Scotts had left, and so I did not know many people. But it was nice to have the opportunity to get back there and work again on my Turkish.

During that long summer vac, Marcus and I went on a work camp, this time in Trabzon, in north-east Turkey. The aim was to help clear up an archaeological site in an old monastery, in Sumer, about twenty kilometres inland from Trabzon. Being on the north coast, and relatively high up, we lived in a thickly

Memories of Turkey

forested area, which was quite cool, and periodically rainy.

During this time, Jos was working in Istanbul, looking after the young children of the British Consul-General, in a magnificent Consulate there. She spent a year there, and really enjoyed it. It was no doubt nice for Ma and Pa to have her relatively close.

Turkey has wonderful memories for me, a place where I learned a lot, and had the opportunity to adjust and prepare for the next stage of life. It was marvelous being able to spend time in Ankara with Ma and Pa, in their and nervous Turkish historian called Ataman. It was the first time he had led a work camp, and was prone to shouting and the camp spirit wasn't as good as the Gaziantep one, but the individual friendships which were struck up more than compensated for this. Our main task was to clear out the ruins of this old monastery, and set aside all the old relics we could find, including painted plaster work which had become detached from the walls and ceilings. At the end of the camp, we left these relics in the monastery, all exposed and unprotected from the eyes of visitors. I learned later that most of these precious relics were pilfered, thus underlying the danger of not having an archaeologist to supervise our work. lovely apartments, and to enjoy the security of their home and an environment where I could develop at my own pace. I obviously obtained a taste for a type of expatriate life, which I subsequently became accustomed to, but as I look back, it was the people I met, both foreign and Turkish, who made the greatest impact, and helped me to gain a much needed self-confidence in myself at that awkward and formative stage between school and university.

Michael Askwith,

23 November 1997

APPENDIX A

COMMUNITY DEVELOPMENT AND LOCAL GOVERNMENT

BY TOM

The pattern of government in more economically developed countries of the world is basically a local government one with the major national responsibilities such as defence and foreign affairs resting with the central government. The rights and privileges of the local authorities have however always been jealously guarded though they have increasingly relied on grants from the central government.

In the developing countries, whereas since time immemorial an informal system of local government suited to the day to day needs of village communities has existed, the major responsibility for government and development has tended to rest with the central government. This has often led to bureaucratic and sometimes autocratic rule. It has tended to slow down development through excessive centralisation, the limitation of the financial resources available due to the State having to bear the major part of the burden, and a lack of cooperation from the rural population owing to their not being concerned with the planning of the programme.

At the same time, in those countries which have not fully developed a cash economy the inhabitants often lack the financial resources to make a system of local government possible. Local government of course presupposes the payment of rates and taxes to the local authority to enable it, with such grants as may be provided by the central government, to meet the cost of most of the services required by the community. The formation of democratic governing bodies representative of the people of the area, the expansion of the economy to enable the community to meet a major part of the expenditure of the local government service, and the delegation of legal responsibilities to enable the authority to control designated local services. Obviously these measures must take time to introduce and can only be implemented by degrees.

It must be accepted that while trained staff are scarce the government has no option but to build up its central services. The danger is however that it may assume that the rate of development must be proportional to the size and resources of the organisation it establishes. Experience shows that this is by no means the case and unless it can involve the rural population in its plans they will not succeed.

In Turkey for instance a very considerable central government organisation has been built up, yet development in the rural areas is disappointingly slow. It is true that as long ago as 1924 the need to develop local government organisations at the village level was forseen and the Village Law promulgated. This, on paper, empowered Village Councils to provide all the services required, but it has not proved effective in practice and the reasons will be examined in due course. Villages with a population of more than 2000 were classed as municipalities and granted a greater degree of autonomy, but have not had any significantly greater success in so far as rural development is concerned. No local government bodies were set up at the Kaza however and those at the Provincial level were not representative of the rural areas.

At the same time, however, the government may be proud of its achievement in obtaining village participation in the provision of most of the village services such as schools, roads, water supplies and community centres. Nevertheless the complaint is still frequently heard from many technical officers that the village people fail to cooperate in carrying out the manual work or to maintain the services provided. This appears to indicate that there is something lacking in the relationship existing between the village people and the government officers.

There is a need to involve the people more closely in the rural development programmes so that they identify themselves with them and work for their success. On the face of it what is required is the introduction of system of local government at the village level. As we have seen however this has been tried and largely failed. The reasons for this appear to be that the constitution of the Village Councils does not always provide for the representation of minority groups. They are not the unifying force which they were intended to be. They have not the financial resources to meet their needs. Since the devaluation of the Lira their revenue has been decimated. They have not the staff to enable them to develop their activities. One clerk has to be shared by up to five villages.

We must, on the other hand, be realistic and recognise that it is not feasible at this stage to establish a formal system of local government in all the 40,000 villages of Turkey. This would involve an immense programme of training and might in the long run merely establish a second bureaucracy at the local level.

Appendix A

Yet examples will be given of village councils which have been guided to become effective organs for development. They have achieved this through following the principles of community development. These examples will indicate that there is room for two types of local government in Turkey at the present time, the one informal at the village level which is synonymous with community development, the other formal at the Kaza and possibly the Nahiya levels.

In the first place there is a need at the village level for the councils established under the Village Law to become fully representative of the village and thereby holding their allegiance. Secondly there is a need for a campaign of enlightenment to make the villagers aware of the benefits they can gain for themselves through their own united efforts, aided by the technical advice of the government and where absolutely necessary its material assistance. There is not space in this paper to explain fully the reasons for these assertions but they will become apparent in the examples given.

Next there is a need for a formal system of local government at the Kaza level representative of the villages as a whole and served by the local technical officers. This body should be responsible for planning the development programme for the area. In the early stages the technical officers might be ex-officio members. Initially the main function of the Kaza Council would be to coordinate the efforts of the technical officers and plan their activities in support of village projects.

It may be that it would not be feasible for every village to appoint a representative for this Council for reasons of distance and expense. In any case the Council would in some large Kazas become unwieldy. Consideration might be given to the establishment of intermediate Councils at the Nahiya level each of which would select a representative for the Kaza Council.

The planning and development of these Councils will take time and it is suggested that they should first start on an experimental basis in selected areas.

To illustrate how these objectives have been realized in various parts of Turkey, examples will now be given of programmes undertaken in a village, a municipality, a Kaza and a Province. These are by no means the only instances of success in this field, but it must be accepted that their number is at present limited.

The village to be described is Dere Sakarya in Bilecik Province. It was one of a number of pilot villages chosen to demonstrate the value of a community

Eyeball to Eyeball

development approach. Two villages were selected in each Kaza, one in a highland and the other in a lowland one. One requirement was that they should be connected by road to the highway so that technical officers might visit them and other villages to see the results of their efforts.

This particular Village built a road five miles long without any help from the government, enclosed the cemetery with a wall, repaired the village community centre so that classes could be organised there and finally collected 100.000 Turkish Liras to build a dam for irrigation purposes. The opening up of the area also enabled the Agricultural Extension Staff to assist farmers to plant fruit trees, no less than 20,000 being planted.

All this was achieved through the formation of a Village Development Council. This was not the same as the official Village Council established by law, and its chairman was not the Muhtar but another leader chosen by the villagers.

Credit, incidentally, for this successful scheme of which Dere Sakarya is only one example must largely go to the Adult Education Chief who persuaded the Governor to launch the scheme. He had been trained in the principles of community development in a seminar which was one of a series organised by the Adult Education Directorate for its staff. The Adult Education Directorate was in fact the first government department to take steps to introduce the concept of community development to Turkey and sent some of its staff to Britain for training.

The second example relates to a village in Kirklareli Province in Thrace named Kaynarca. This is in fact a municipality having more than 2000 inhabitants and enjoying a greater degree of autonomy.

The village schoolmaster was elected Mayor and he devoted all his efforts to persuade the villagers to collect money to compensate a mill owner and make use of the stream he used to irrigate some 600 hectares of land five kilometres from the village and grow rice. It took a great deal of persuasion, but the villagers eventually agreed to find the 100.000 Turkish Lira required, though they only achieved this by selling some of their cattle. They then dug the canal without any government help. The government gave them technical advice about the lay out of the irrigation works. In the first year they reaped a crop worth a million and a half Turkish Lira but had to send it to Istanbul for milling. This year they are building their own mill and will save large sums of money as a result. They are now, encouraged by their success, planning to acquire the rights of two more mills and irrigate additional land. They also have ideas of building a hotel and a cinema and installing a drinking water system.

Appendix A

Incidentally they had previously bought a pump to irrigate another area for the cultivation of sugar beet and with the proceeds borrowed money for the installation of an electricity supply.

Here then is a clear case of community development methods being used to improve the economy of the municipality. The dividing line between community development and local government is in fact very narrow. The interesting part about this remarkable achievement is that the government was scarcely involved. The school teacher led the campaign in his capacity as Mayor and the government only gave technical advice and no material assistance apart from loans.

The next example concerns the Kaza of Altinözü in Hatay Province. This was one of the Project Areas chosen by the State Planning Organisation to experiment in the planned introduction of community development in various parts of Turkey.

This project is interesting not so much from its physical achievements, but the organisational pattern evolved. In the first year of operation, after a series of seminars for government, 24 villages were chosen for intensive development. Courses were organized for Muhtars, village leaders, priests and school teachers and the Village Councils expanded in each case to make them more representative. A committee was set up at the Kaza level to coordinate the work of the technical officers. This committee considered, together with representatives of the various villages included in the scheme, their development plans. Here then was the germ of the idea suggested earlier of a local government body at the Kaza level.

A number of the projects concerned the individual needs of the different villages, a school here, a bridge there, shops in another. Another scheme involved the construction of a road 36 Kms long, which would link thirteen villages with the main highway to enable them to export their olive crop. This scheme had been urged for some years but the different villages had failed to agree. It was only when the expanded Village Councils and the Kaza Committee were set up that agreement was reached. Many farmers gave up land and olive trees to construct the road.

160.000 Turkish Lira were collected to pay for the fuel and drivers wages of the road building machinery. This incidentally was more than was contributed for roads by all the other seven Kazas of the Province. The road is now complete and the Kaza Committee is turning its attention to the installation of an olive oil press to improve the quality of the local product, and to the setting up of marketing cooperatives to increase the return on the crop.

Here is an example of community development laying the foundation for a local authority at the Kaza level. Moreover the Kaza had the support of a local government fund at the Provincial level and a further link in the chain is therefore being forged. This year the remaining villages in the Kaza are being incorporated in the scheme.

The fourth example is of a scheme in the Edirne Province. In this area the Director of Health saw the need for mother and child clinics at which the midwives would be based. Through a health education campaign conducted by men who had previously been employed in a successful malaria eradication scheme no less than eighty Village Councils were persuaded to build the Health Centres. They received no assistance from government apart from furniture.

Here then is an example of a scheme on a Provincial basis built up on the foundation of existing Village Councils. Efforts are being made now to broaden the base of development through the selection of the Central Kaza as a community development project.

What are the lessons of these examples. First of all they all owe their success to the promotion of Village Councils. In some cases they were those established under the Village Law, in others they have been modified or expanded.

Secondly they have depended upon inspired leadership of some individual. In the case of the village it was largely the Adult Education Chief. In the case of the Municipality the school teacher Mayor. In that of the Kaza the Kaymakam. In the Provincial scheme the Director of Health.

Thirdly none of them received much material aid from the government. Success was achieved more by stimulation of local initiative and the provision of technical assistance.

Fourthly, and of greatest importance, they indicate the latent ability of the village people to organise and undertake substantial development activities at considerable personal sacrifice.

These lessons and experiences have been gained in widely separated parts of Turkey and are sufficient to justify the belief that the methods could be applied with success throughout the country.

Appendix A

We should now consider what steps the government is taking to make use of the experience gained so far and expand the area of activities.

The Ministry of Village Affairs has been formed specifically to improve village life through community development methods. It incorporates the Adult Education Directorate and the Group from the State Planning Organisation who have been the bodies mainly concerned with the introduction of community development in Turkey. It combines most of the agencies of informal education required to convert the village people to a desire for progress and the adoption of new ways of life. It is establishing a coordinating organisation from the Ministerial to the Village level. Committees will be established to coordinate the activities of the Ministries, the Directors in the Provinces, the technical officers at the Kazas and the inhabitants and front line workers in the villages. Moreover the villagers will be represented on the Kaza and Provincial Councils by the inclusion of members of various bodies working in the rural areas such as cooperative societies, village road unions and betterment associations. Training institutions for government officers and village leaders are being planned at the National and Provincial levels. Universities are being encouraged to set up Institutes of Community Development.

All the different parts are therefore to be found within the Ministry to build the machinery to motivate a widespread programme. It is true that the link with any plan to promote a system of local government is at present somewhat obscure, but the Ministry is geared to expand its activities to introduce it as a logical consequence.

The experience of the various experiments so far conducted either by the village people independently of government, or by various official agencies, appears to suggest the following. That the best results should be achieved by the development of a system of informal local government at the village level by community development methods and the establishment of a more formal system at the Kaza level. Greater attention will have to be given to the local authorities at the Kaza level to ensure full representation of the villages. Intermediate Councils at the Nahiye level either to take charge of certain services or to operate as Electoral Colleges for the Kaza Councils may be desirable.

Your Faculty has always taken a keen interest in these problems and have already made a notable contribution to the actual introduction of the new concept in the rural areas. You may feel that studies of the experience acquired and recommendations on the future policy to be adopted may be worth your

Eyeball to Eyeball

while. There is no doubt that any work you decide to do in this field will be extremely valuable.

What appears to be needed more than anything else is to spread a knowledge of what has actually been achieved, even though this is at present on a limited scale, and disappointing in certain areas. The general public and certainly the world at large is insufficiently aware of these remarkable achievements, and still less of the possibilities of extending them on a much wider scale. The key to success is available whatever sceptics may say.

A last suggestion must be made with all deference, and that is that it appears likely that more progress in rural development through the fostering of local institutions will be achieved by basing policy on the traditions and experience of the past than by trying out too many experiments in new methods. The basic structure and personnel are there at the Village and Kaza levels if they can only be harnessed to the chariot of progress. There seems too much defeatism and lack of confidence in the ability of village leaders and field officers to alter the rural face of Turkey. This is certainly not justified and if all concerned can be united in a common aim there is no doubt that great things can be done.

Above all, those out in the country areas, whether officials or village leaders, who are doing such good work, need all the encouragement and support that we can give them whether by visits, publicity or material help.

Community Development Evaluation Advisor, Turkish Ministry of Villages Affairs.

COMMUNITY DEVELOPMENT IN TURKEY

BY TOM

Little has been written on the community development programme which has been built up in Turkey over the last few years. Considerable progress has been made in certain areas and the methods adopted to bring this about will no doubt be of interest to those working in this field in countries with similar characteristics, particularly the Mohammedan countries of the Middle East. This programme really stems from the establishment of the present government in 1960 and the new spirit that permeated it. On the other hand the origins go far deeper than that, to the early days of Mustafa Kemal Atatürk, in fact, when in 1924 he introduced the Village Law.

Appendix A

THE BACKGROUND

It is therefore necessary to provide the background of this interesting experiment in rural development. First of all we must appreciate the vastness of Turkey, geographically rather than in terms of population. It is one tenth the size of Europe with a population of thirty million people. It stretches from the borders of Bulgaria and Greece at the Western end of the Black Sea, to the mountains along the Russian and Iranian borders, 1700 miles to the East. Its mean width between the Black and Mediterranean Seas is 500 miles. In the centre lies the vast and almost treeless Anatolian Plain of rolling grass land. This is bounded on every side by mountains which pile up in a great massif covering the whole Eastern end of the country. Between the mountains and the sea the land is fertile, but the Anatolian Plain is drier and more suitable for sheep rearing and the cultivation of wheat.

Turkey has of course a prodigious history and civilized communities have existed there for more than six thousand years. Almost annually discoveries of ever older cultures are made. But for all that, until quite recent times, the pattern of life in the rural areas has remained largely unchanged. Methods of cultivation in many areas are still those of biblical times. It is these conditions that, mainly since the establishment of the Republic under Mustafa Kemal Atatürk, great efforts are being made to change and modernize.

THE FIRST STEP

The first step taken in 1924 was the introduction of the Village Law which aimed at establishing local government bodies at the village level. These local authorities had certain responsibilities to maintain good government in the villages. They were also empowered to encourage voluntary village communal effort to improve local conditions.

Although these local authorities succeeded in enlisting the participation of the villages in the building of schools, the construction of roads, and the provision of water supplies, they were not so effective in stimulating initiative and a sense of purpose in the village communities. The village councils often failed to represent the whole community of the village, which was divided and at odds. The devaluation of the Turkish lira reduced the revenue which the local authorities were empowered to collect from the inhabitants, and thus restricted their activities.

Eyeball to Eyeball

VILLAGE INSTITUTES

Meanwhile, a drive to spread enlightenment through Village Institutes was organized and this was undoubtedly effective in awakening the dormant rural population. In the early 1950's these Village Institutes were discontinued, however.

These Village Institutes have had a much greater influence than is always appreciated. Their purpose was to train the teachers of the Village Primary Schools in a very comprehensive manner to enable them to have an influence on all aspects of village life. Of greater importance, however, was the way that they succeeded in giving the teachers a sense of public service. Many of those trained in the Village Institutes are today still doing outstanding work in the villages in the true spirit of community development.

AGRICULTURAL EXTENSION

After the last war considerable foreign aid was provided to Turkey, much of it in the form of farm machinery. The Agricultural Extension Service was formed and many of its members were given training abroad. Credit was provided for the provision of fertilizers.

All these measures had the effect of increasing productivity, but they were not enough. The bulk of the rural population remained poor and many migrated to the towns to seek employment in the new industries which were being established. Turkey became almost self-sufficient in so far as the manufacture of its domestic requirements were concerned, but relied heavily on foreign loans to achieve this.

THE PROMOTION OF RURAL DEVELOPMENT

After the 1960 Revolution a new awareness of the need to promote rural, as opposed to industrial, development became apparent. What is more, thoughtful people began to recognize the importance of stimulating popular initiative in the villages and to reverse the tendency of an excessive reliance on the government in all development activities. Those concerned with rural development began to study the experience of other countries in this field.

The effect of this new awareness was felt not only among government agencies and field officers, but among the village people themselves. On the one hand government field officers launched schemes which depended upon village initiative and voluntary participation. On the other, village communities began

Appendix A

to establish associations for mutual assistance to construct schools, roads, mosques and the marketing of agricultural produce.

ADULT EDUCATION AND COMMUNITY DEVELOPMENT

At this stage, the Adult Education Directorate began to interest itself in community development. It sent members of its staff to the United Kingdom for training. It organized Seminars for Education staff throughout the country. Certain Adult Education Officers then began to persuade Governors to launch schemes of community development in their areas. Some of these have been very effective and will be described later.

THE FIVE YEAR PLAN

Then in 1962 the State Planning Organization framed the First Five Year Plan for national development. A scheme of community development through the establishment of Pilot Areas was incorporated in the Plan. Six Projects would be launched annually in different Provinces and by 1967 it was planned to cover all the 67 Provinces of Turkey. During the ensuing ten years these Projects, each of which would initially comprise a sub-Province, would be extended to cover the whole country. A group of specialists was formed in the State Planning Office who were made responsible to guide Provincial Officers in the launching of the Projects. Community Development Seminars were organized for Governors and Sub-Governors on a Regional basis.

Some of the schemes have been successful where the principles of community development were understood and applied. Others have been disappointing.

SPONTANEOUS SCHEMES OF COMMUNITY DEVELOPMENT

In the meanwhile a number of individual schemes of community development were undertaken independently. Sometimes they were sponsored by a government department, sometimes by a Kaymakam or sub-Provincial Governor, sometimes by some public-spirited individual. In each case the village council was stimulated to enlist popular support for the project which might be an irrigation scheme, a road, a theatre or even a series of mother and child welfare centres. Increased interest became apparent among government field officers in the possibilities of this new approach to rural development problems.

One should mention at this stage that although the machinery of government for enlisting popular initiative or support for development schemes was inadequate, a traditional practice of mutual assistance has existed since time immemorial. This system not only provided the means by which harvesting or house building could be carried out economically and easily, but also for the provision of community services. This has been the means whereby the people have solved their domestic problems for centuries. When the government sought to enlist the people's participation in the construction of schools, roads and water supplies, it unfortunately misused this traditional system. Instead of leaving the organization to the traditional leaders it directed the activities of the voluntary groups towards the projects which it desired to promote. This gave a bad name to the traditional system and the term describing it can no longer be used to express the meaning of community development.

THE PROBLEMS

In the meanwhile the majority of administrative and technical officers maintained their traditional paternalistic and authoritarian attitude. They had little confidence in the ability of villagers to solve their own problems with the technical assistance of government. Other factors also inhibited popular development activities, chief among which was the unequal pattern of land ownership. The majority of villagers had either no land or inadequate land for a decent livelihood. These people had to engage in share-cropping on the land of wealthy landlords or in agricultural and urban employment. There were however, many services which all the villagers needed, whether they owned sufficient land or not, and they could often be persuaded to participate in providing them. Such services included the construction of schools, water supplies and village industries.

But the main problem was, and continues to be, the conversion of the attitude of government field officers; to persuade them to adopt a sympathetic and understanding attitude towards village aspirations; to convince them of the need for enlightenment among village communities if they are to be persuaded to adopt new and modern methods of agriculture, animal husbandry or the preservation of health. This is the principal task of those who are charged with the responsibility for community development in Turkey and they are tackling it through seminars, conferences and publications. It is believed by many, however, that the conservative elements will only be converted through practical examples of the successful application of community development measures. Such examples are increasing in number and steps are being taken to inform the public about them. They are, however, little known even in Turkey, let alone in the outside world, and therefore the following accounts may be of interest to readers.

Appendix A

EXAMPLES OF PROGRAMMES

To illustrate the different methods adopted in various parts of Turkey, examples will now be given of programmes undertaken in a village, a municipality, a kaza, and a Province. These are by no means the only instances of success in this field, but it must be acknowledged that their number is at present limited.

The village to be described is Dere Sakarya in Bilecik Province. It was one of a number of pilot villages chosen to demonstrate the value of a community development approach. Two villages were selected in each Kaza, one in a highland and the other in a lowland area. One requirement was that they should be connected by road to the highway so that technical officers might visit them and the other villages see the results of their efforts.

This particular village built a road five miles long without any help from the government, enclosed the cemetery with a wall, repaired the village community centre so that classes could be organized there and finally collected L4,000 to build a dam for irrigation purposes. The opening up of the area also enabled the Agricultural Extension Staff to assist farmers to plant fruit trees. No less than 20,000 were planted.

All this was achieved through the formation of a Village Development Council. This was not the same as the official Village Council established by law, and its chairman was not the Muktar but another leader chosen by the villagers.

Credit, incidentally, for this successful scheme of which Dere Sakarya village is only one example must largely go to the Adult Education Chief who persuaded the Governor to launch the scheme. He had been trained in the principles of community development in a seminar which was one of a series organized by the Adult Education Directorate.

The second example relates to a village in Kirklareli Province in Thrace, named Kaynaca. This is in fact a municipality having more than 2,000 inhabitants and enjoying a greater degree of autonomy.

The village schoolmaster was elected Mayor and he devoted all his efforts to persuade the villagers to collect money to compensate a mill owner and make use of the stream he used, to irrigate some 600 hectares of land three miles from the village and grow rice. It took a great deal of persuasion, but the villagers eventually agreed to find the L4,000 required, though they only achieved this by selling some of their cattle. They then dug the canal without any government help. The government gave them technical advice about the layout of the

Eyeball to Eyeball

irrigation works. In the first year they reaped a crop worth L60,000, but had to send it to Istanbul for milling. This year they are building their own mill and will save large sums of money as a result. They are now, encouraged by their success, planning to acquire the rights of two more mills and irrigate additional land. They also have ideas of building a hotel and a cinema and installing a drinking water system. Incidentally, they had previously bought a pump to irrigate another area for the cultivation of sugar beet, and with the proceeds borrowed money for the installation of an electricity supply.

Here then is a clear case of community development methods being used to improve the economy of the municipality. The dividing line between community development and local government is in fact very narrow. The interesting part about this remarkable achievement is that the government was scarcely involved. The school teacher led the campaign in his capacity as Mayor and the government only gave technical advice and no material assistance, apart from loans.

The next example concerns the Kaza of Altinozu in Hatay Province. This was one of the Project Areas chosen by the State Planning Organization to experiment in the planned introduction of community development in various parts of Turkey.

This project is interesting not so much from its physical achievements, but the organizational pattern evolved. In the first year of operation, after a series of seminars for government officials to orientate them to the idea of community development, twenty four villages were chosen for intensive development. Courses were organized for Muktars, village leaders, priests, and school teachers and the Village Councils were expanded in each case to make them more representative.

A committee was set up at the Kaza level to coordinate the work of the technical officers. This committee considered, together with representatives of the various villages included in the scheme, their development plans.

A number of the projects concerned the individual needs of the different villages, a school here, a bridge there, shops in another. Another scheme involved the construction of a road 35 kilometres long, which would link thirteen villages with the main highway to enable them to export their olive crop. This scheme had been urged for some years, but the different villages had failed to agree. It was only when the expanded Village Councils and the Kaza Committee were set up that agreement was reached.

Appendix A

Many farmers gave up land and olive trees to construct the road. L6,000 was collected to pay for the fuel and driver's wages of the road-building machinery. This, incidentally, was more than was contributed for roads by all the other seven Kazas of the Province. The road is now complete and the Kaza Committee is turning its attention to the installation of an olive oil press to improve the quality of the local product, and to the setting up of marketing cooperatives to increase the return on the crop.

The fourth example is of a scheme in the Edirne Province. In this area the Director of Health saw the need for mother and childcare clinics at which the midwives would be based. Through a health education campaign conducted by men who had previously been employed in a successful malaria eradication scheme no less than eighty Village Councils were persuaded to build Health Centres. They received no assistance from government apart from furniture.

Here then is an example of a scheme on a Provincial basis built up on the foundation of existing Village Councils. Efforts are being made now to broaden the base of development through the selection of the Central Kaza as a community development project.

THE LESSONS LEARNT

What are the lessons of these examples? First of all they all owe their success to the promotion of Village Councils. In some cases they were those established under the Village Law, in others they have been modified or expanded.

Secondly, they have depended upon inspired leadership of some individual. In the case of the village, it was largely the Adult Education Chief; in the case of the municipality, the school teacher Mayor, in that of the Kaza the Kaymakam; in the Provincial scheme, the Director of Health.

Thirdly, none of them received much material aid from the government. Success was achieved more by stimulation of local initiative and the provision of technical advice.

Fourthly, and of greatest importance, they indicate the latent ability of the village people of Turkey to organize and undertake substantial development activities at considerable personal sacrifice.

These lessons and experiences have been gained in widely separated parts of Turkey, and are sufficient to justify the belief that the methods could be applied with success throughout the country.

We should now consider what steps the government is taking to make use of the experience gained so far and expand the area of activities.

THE MINISTRY OF VILLAGE AFFAIRS

The Ministry of Village Affairs has been formed specifically to improve village life through community development methods. It incorporates the Adult Education Directorate and the Group from the State Planning Organization, which have been the bodies mainly concerned with the introduction of community development in Turkey. It combines most of the agencies of informal education required to convert the village people to a desire for progress and the adoption of new ways of life. It is establishing a coordinating organization from the Ministerial to the village levels. Committees will be established to coordinate the activities of the various Ministries, the Directors in the Provinces, the technical officers at the Kazas and the inhabitants and front line workers in the villages. Moreover the villagers will be represented on the Kaza and Provincial Councils by the inclusion of members of various bodies working in the rural areas such as cooperative societies, Village road unions and betterment associations. Training institutions for government officers and village leaders are being planned at the National and Provincial levels. Universities are being encouraged to set up Institutes of Community Development.

So it is clear that a movement is afoot which may have far reaching consequences to the economic and social wellbeing of the rural areas of Turkey and be of significance beyond its boundaries.

Glossary

Bokhari	Stove in living room
Boyaci	Shoe cleaners
Chadri	Cloak
Chai Khonas	Tea shop
Dolmus	Shared taxi
Eskiji	Second hand dealers
Gechikundo	Self-built housing
Garis	Cabs
Gul-khona	Conservatories
Iskender kebab	Named after Alexander the Great
Jeshan	Spring festival
Jui	Water course
Karakol	Skin of unborn calf
Lokanta	Tea shop
Nan	Unleavened bread
Purdah	Lit: "Tent" concealing garment
Suk	Market
Top Kapi	Treasury in Istanbul
Toplum kalkum mase	Self-help projects
Vali	Governor
Yamurtas	Egg seller